Praise for *Writing Without a Parac...*

This book has something most instruction completely misses: a practical set of exercises and explanations to help with the imaginative act of original composition. It will be useful for beginners, superb for writers in the middle of their training and an absolute lifesaver for pros who have lost their nerve. Written as if a knowledgable friend is chatting to you about your creative processes, this is a book of encouragement in that most lonely of tasks. It is a mate to sit on the arm of your chair and cheer you on as you go. I shall recommend it to all my students and many of my friends.

Mimi Thebo, Senior Lecturer in Creative Writing, Bath Spa University

Freefall is an amazing process that unlocks the writing and ignites the inspiration. I'm always telling anyone who wants to write: do Freefall! Here, as in the workshops, Barbara is its skilled facilitator and trustworthy guide.

Helena McEwen, author of *The Big House* and *Invisible River* (Bloomsbury)

Here is a book which charts new territory. With its injunction to "go fearward", Writing Without a Parachute *invites the writer to fall with confidence into the ether of the creative self in order to write with skill and authenticity; above all, to write better. With a wealth of examples from life-writing, fiction and poetry, Barbara Turner-Vesselago demonstrates the effectiveness of this unique and exciting approach which will be of value for writers, mentors and facilitators alike.*

Louise Green, Editor, *Lapidus Journal*

Life force not used becomes morbid – yet we all have a muse in us. Writing Without a Parachute *is such a goldmine of insight and inspiration for learning how to sing out your muse, even if only for yourself. Read this book whether you want to be a professional writer or more likely, someone – basically all of us – who needs to find and hear their own voice – and let it flow – so that your life will also flow.*

Richard Moss, author of *The Mandala of Being* and *Inside-Out Healing*

Writing Without a Parachute

by the same author

Freefall into Fiction
Finding Form
Barbara Turner-Vesselago
ISBN 978 1 78592 172 8
eISBN 978 1 78450 442 7

of related interest

Writing Routes
A Resource Handbook of Therapeutic Writing
Gillie Bolton, Victoria Field and Kate Thompson
Foreword by Gwyneth Lewis
ISBN 978 1 84905 107 1
eISBN 978 0 85700 303 4
Writing for Therapy or Personal Development

Writing Without a Parachute

The Art of Freefall

Barbara Turner-Vesselago

Jessica Kingsley *Publishers*
London and Philadelphia

Excerpt from *Strong Voices: Conversations with 50 Canadian authors* by Alan Twigg is
reprinted with the permission of Harbour Publishing, 1988, www.harbourpublishing.com

First published by Vala Publishing Co-operative Ltd, UK in 2013

This edition first published in 2017
by Jessica Kingsley Publishers
73 Collier Street
London N1 9BE, UK
and
400 Market Street, Suite 400
Philadelphia, PA 19106, USA

www.jkp.com

Library of Congress Cataloging in Publication Data
A CIP catalog record for this book is available from the Library of Congress

British Library Cataloguing in Publication Data
A CIP catalogue record for this book is available from the British Library
ISBN 978 1 78592 171 1
eISBN 978 1 78450 443 4

Printed and bound in Great Britain

Acknowledgements

Throughout this book, I have spoken as if I have done things on my own when in fact everything I have ever accomplished has been so much the result of loving support from other people:

Three extraordinary mentors, who have both changed me and inspired my way of teaching: Professor John Pengwerne Matthews, novelist W.O. Mitchell, and physician, writer and seminar leader, Dr Richard Moss. The first two, now deceased, not only believed in me far more than I believed in myself, but also brought me to a whole new understanding of how writing works, in academia and in fiction. Richard Moss, who continues to lead people to the edge of themselves in his seminars and retreats with generosity and integrity, has been for almost thirty years a blessing in my life. I am grateful, too, for his tireless quest to find words for the Unnameable, many of which have found their way into my own vocabulary over the years.

My dear friend, writer Diana Kiesners, who in her role as publisher conceived, edited, designed and (together with Maria Gould (now Maria Meindl) at The Writing Space) published my 50-page introductory book, *Freefall: Writing Without a Parachute*.

Beloved friends around the world with whom I feel utterly and always welcome: Megan Grace, Marigold and Richard Farmer, and

Maxine Martin in England, Nicki and Jacob de Hoog, Kaye Gersch, and the late Margaret Curl in Australia. Devon Ronner, Lelle Taffyn, Rosemary Stevens, Nicola-Jane LeBreton, Julie Gittus, Bob Thornhill, Sandra Jensen and Geoff Mead – all former students who have become friends – have supported my work and me in ways too numerous to mention, as have their partners.

All the people who come forward to organise the workshops and make the continuation of this work possible – you know who you are; I know what it takes for you to do this, and I am so grateful.

Miriam Swadron for all the encouragement, and Christopher Brightman, for reading the manuscript and for being there, at Cambridge as now. Clare Bolton for working on permissions. Julia Press, for all you give, to everyone who knows you.

Sarah Bird, editor extraordinaire, whose work is so gifted and whose presence, even by email, such a gift. Peter Reason, whose assistance with editing I have found both wise and helpful. Alan Blakemore, who copy-edited this book, Kay Russell and Denis Kennedy, who proofread it, Michaela Meadow, who designed it, Iva Carrdus, who is marketing it: such skilled and friendly people, so good at what they do. O brave old world, that has such people in it!

Above all, my beloved husband, Michael Vesselago, whose insight and editing advice have been such a boon to me throughout this process. Thank you for so enthusiastically discussing every little aspect of this book's evolution, as you always do, everything that matters to me.

To all my students, past and present: their courage,
their dedication, and their writing.

And to our cousin Sandy (Alexander Alexandrovich Zvegintzov),
who died climbing a mountain – one of so many.

Contents

Contents

Introduction

"How can I get past whatever's stopping me from writing?" "I know I have a book in me, but how can I get it out?" "I feel as if I'm bobbing along on the surface when I write. How can I go deeper?" "Writing has gone stale for me." "I can't get started!" "Is there any way I can stop struggling with my writing and start to enjoy it?"

Virtually everyone I have ever worked with has been contending with at least one of these writing dilemmas – from experienced writers to people who have never even tried to write but have always thought they would. And I hear almost daily from others who are wrestling – often in some desperation – with the same problems: why can't I do this? Why is it so hard?

The fact that I hear these questions asked so often is not in itself surprising. Writing creatively is, after all, an activity you can practise on your own. Writers have been doing so for centuries. People don't seek out writing teachers unless they have a problem. What is surprising is the fact that despite the voracity of readers, despite the variety of ways now available to publish writing, and despite the number of books offering writing advice, this current of desperation continues to swell. "I want to write, but something is stopping me. I just can't seem to make it happen."

What I have come to understand, in working with people's writing for almost three decades in half-a-dozen English-speaking countries around the world, is that it doesn't matter how strong the will to write may be, or how much knowledge about the craft of writing you have: if you want to write creatively all of this has to be balanced by the ability to surrender.

By surrender, I don't mean handing over your power to someone or something and becoming a victim. I mean learning how to allow your willing, intending self to get out of the way, so that a deeper level of vulnerability becomes possible. In this "surrendered" way of writing, you become truly present for what comes up as you write, with an open heart, able to let things emerge on the page that you didn't anticipate. You may find you're able to convey human complexity at a depth that surprises you, or proceed on the basis of insights you didn't know you'd had. You may realise that you've entered the world you're creating so deeply that it feels like a lucid dream – or that may not turn out to be the way your mind works at all. The specifics of what will happen are unpredictable; they will be uniquely your own. But what I can predict is that you will begin to see that, though they both use language, writing in this way is not the same as thinking. It can take you to different places from those you can reach by thinking. It proceeds by its own logic, and seems to draw on a greater range of thought, feeling and invention than it is possible to gain access to in ordinary waking life.

One way to conceive of this comparison is to think of writing in this open, surrendered way as relaxing the tight grip of the rational, egoic self in order to gain access to a deeper field of awareness that is, in the main, unconscious. Of course there are communications back and forth between that deeper awareness and the habitual thought-processes of our daily lives, but they often manifest as brief flashes of what we call intuition, or insight, perhaps. Like meditation, writing in this way seems to develop a stronger bridge from the rational mind, with which we are all too numbingly familiar, to the less well known potential. Seen from the point of view of the rational mind, much of what you write in this way may not seem to you to be of much value at first. And that's why I talk about "getting out of your own way" – it's a matter of quieting the objections of one part of the mind so that what this more unbounded awareness has to contribute can make itself known.

In the book that follows, I will be providing you with a reliable way of finding this essential vulnerability, a method you can use until that has become central to the way you write. In the early chapters, you will be given the precepts of Freefall Writing,[1] which offer a dependable means of shifting into it. These chapters both explore what the precepts mean and show you how to remain aware of them as you do the writing suggested there. Building on what you will have accomplished by doing that writing, the later chapters show you certain important ways the scope of the precepts can be extended.

If you are willing to write and to follow those precepts, then no matter what your level of experience, you can discover the degree of absorption and spontaneity that good writing requires. And once you can reliably depend on doing so – once you have learned, in other words, to get out of your own way and let the writing lead you – you can begin to learn to bring intention back into the balance, directing that spontaneity in such a way that it serves your specific writing goals.

The one catch, though, for readers of this book, is that you do have to *do* the writing. If you just read what I have to say, intending to write sometime, you'll only be adding to your store of will and intention, which is probably already bursting at the seams. "But nobody does the exercises in a writing book!" a writer friend protested when I mentioned this necessity. Nonetheless. This book, which distils much of what I have been doing with writers in person these past three decades, has been written to support you in restoring an essential balance to the writing process. It is as important that you write as it is that you read the examples I have given (which one student called "learning to write by osmosis"). Without your deepening your understanding of this process *through writing* as you go, much of what I say (and even why I say it) won't make the necessary kind of sense to you. Remember: *writing* (in this surrendered, "Freefall" way) *is not the same as thinking*. It has its own logic and its own power – both greater than and different from the power of your rational, thinking mind. The only way to learn about these differences is to experience them.

Chapter One
Finding the Way

In the chapters that follow, you will find a very practical guide to "writing without a parachute", to finding the deeper level of trust in writing that comes from what I have called "surrender". It's from that deeper level of trust that everything else you need to know about writing will follow. But before you begin, I think it might be useful for me to describe how I, personally, came to understand the connection between the kind of open-hearted vulnerability I'm talking about, and good writing.

Discovering Surrender

Have you ever been caught off-guard, as a child, if not as an adult, by a moment when everything fell into place and you seemed to be guided by a knowing that lay deeper than your conscious mind, or beyond the familiar bounds of what you knew as your ordinary "self"?

I was impelled toward much of what I now know about writing by one such experience – so prolonged and intense that it made me question everything I thought I knew. Was it an experience of psychosis? Or was it simply an experience of opening into a different way of seeing and knowing that lay within my own mind? All I know is that it left me very differently attuned to the world, and unabashedly curious about how the mind works. Partly because it happened while I was stranded in the midst of a demanding writing project – and primarily because one of my deepest ambitions had always been to write, that experience led me, step by step, to find out what I needed to know about how writing works, and how I could learn to do it.

I was several years into the study of modern literature and critical theory for a doctoral thesis at the University of Cambridge, when I contracted an illness (Bell's Palsy) that put a stop to my formal research for a while. I had been reading voraciously up to that point, but I hadn't been able to make myself write much yet. Now, to the mounting distress I felt about the thesis was added the well-founded fear that I might end up permanently disfigured by this disease. I suppose the combined force of these powerful anxieties must somehow have overwhelmed my customary controls.

As I began to recover from the virus, I became aware that whatever constituted my familiar sense of "self" was beginning to slip. I would become almost unbearably anxious, or wildly excited, or, even more disconcerting, have episodes of feeling as if the world were moving past me like a film, but I wasn't there. I was still taking medication for the virus, so I tried to tell myself these were just side effects. Then I finished the pills, but the side effects continued. At that point, I fell into real terror, certain that I was losing my mind.

During paralysing bouts of panic, I promised myself I would check into the local psychiatric hospital: I'd do whatever it took to make this stop. But once the panic had ebbed, I'd tell myself, "Walk through the fire", a phrase I thought I'd seen in Doris Lessing's novel, *The Golden Notebook*, the only thing I had ever read about a nervous breakdown. To me those words meant that perhaps, if I could just keep going, I would somehow come out the other side.

Then one early morning, as I stood in the kitchen watching the sun come up at the bottom of the garden, I began to feel as if the sun were pouring through the space between my ribs. It was as if the whole of creation were streaming through the middle of my body. I was it and it was me; there was only this ceaseless becoming. Clearly, it had always been this way. I had just never known it before. This contravened the entire structure of my familiar, "intentional" self. Like it or not, I had somehow accidentally stumbled on a whole new (to me) aspect of being alive.

And like it I did. I strongly felt – it was palpable – that this endlessly streaming energy of creation wasn't neutral. It was positive and beneficent. It wasn't personal, and it certainly didn't care about me personally. It just was, I was part of it, and it was good.

For weeks I stayed immersed in this blissful new awareness, re-evaluating everything I had thought I knew in the light of it. So many phrases I had heard before without really understanding them made perfect sense to me now. Was this "the peace that passeth understanding"? And I knew that if I had discovered this much about this fundamental truth of existence, there must be so many people out there who knew infinitely more.

From time to time, a bolt of fear shot through me: was I actually now totally insane?

I longed to spend a year or two just exploring this new understanding. But how? I still had to eat and pay the rent, and for that I had my Fellowship Committee to satisfy. They wanted to know how the dissertation was going. In all the time I had spent at Cambridge, I had managed to write only fifty knotted-up pages, endlessly revised. Right now I could hardly read, let alone marshal arguments for a thesis. I managed a few stilted paragraphs to satisfy the Committee about what I was (in theory) writing, and tried to put this streaming sense of oneness on the back burner, hoping I could still allow it to come through in my life in whatever ways it would.

Now that I had known the world, not as an object with myself as subject, but as a constantly unfolding stream of which I was a part, the whole notion of creativity had taken on a new importance for me. I could see that in some way writers – artists of any kind – must mediate between this spontaneous evolving that I now experienced as part of my being, and their own design. That had to be what they were doing; the evidence was all around me, in literature, in music. But how could they take part in one without losing the other? That question now lay at the heart, for me, of how to live – of what a human being could be.

I had been preparing myself for a life in academia: analysing and generalising about books that had already been written. Did I really want to spend my time this way? Even the task of arguing my thesis (about Virginia Woolf's aesthetic theory) seemed to demand that I go back to an earlier, much more constrained way of thought.

I found myself yearning to write, but not in an academic way. I wanted to come closer to the fire, to take part in the *process of creativity* itself, by writing, and I longed to find out more about how to do this. Maybe I should just get away from the thesis for a while. A university in Canada wrote to offer me a lectureship in literature, but instead, I applied to a university in Africa. I told myself that if I tried teaching literature to people who didn't have a longstanding academic tradition, they wouldn't take its value for granted, and I could find out what it actually meant to them. Perhaps seeing that would change my mind. A deeper and more secret motive lay in how afraid I felt of going somewhere I knew nothing about, and where I knew no-one. Facing into the fear when I had felt I was going insane in Cambridge had led to what I now thought of as a "nervous breakthrough"; perhaps doing what I was afraid to do now would once again provide the key to a hidden door.

So it did, but for very different reasons than the ones I had anticipated. My fears about being alone came to nothing: I could not have gone to a friendlier, more welcoming place. Nigeria was also the last place to find out about the value of studying literature. I quickly discovered that most of my students had long ago given up assuming that anything they studied would have any relevance to their lives whatsoever. They would do what we asked them to do to earn their degrees, but that was all. So I moved on (insofar as the course structure would allow it) to encouraging them to write themselves – and there the learning lay.

To my amazement, I found that the same students who loved to talk and joke their way through seminars on literature could and would, delightedly, focus on writing for hours at a time. Their writing seemed to pour out, molten, in an uninhibited and highly readable way. If anything partook of that boundless energy of becoming, this did. And far from being chaotic or formless, much of what they wrote was as absorbing to read as they had found it to write in the first place. Some of them even had novels they wrote in our sessions published in the "African novel series" that several major publishers were scouting for at the time. I kept thinking, if only I could write that way!

What I learned from these students about writing seemed incontrovertible. They wrote with an ease I could only dream about, possibly *because* they had no tradition of intellectual abstraction. They didn't plan or theorise about what they were going to write. They simply wrote and didn't stop themselves, and their writing flowed, free of intellectualised intentions. My own skills in analysing and predicting, as well as the thousand things I already "knew" about writing from studying literature, were doing nothing to help me; in fact, they only seemed to hinder. My students' spontaneity and focused absorption was what I craved, but all I seemed to have learned through years of study was how to interrupt myself.

For almost five years, I stayed in Nigeria, teaching literature, and learning from my writing students. I had time – and something in the relaxed and forgiving quality of life there was hugely helpful to this – to incubate my experience and intuitions about life, the creative process, and writing. So much had come to my students just by writing as they had. *Wanting only to be absorbed*, they had evolved whole worlds, and with them, quite a remarkable degree of skill in writing. All I had to do, really, came after the fact: to promote the parts that worked the best, and help them trim some of the excess. Surely this was a way of writing – and teaching writing – that would have a great deal to offer, whatever the writer wanted it to accomplish in the long run.

But the flow of events in the rest of my world pushed me forward. I realised that I would have to leave Africa, and what I was learning about writing and the creative process, to take the next step. Time was running out for me to submit my thesis. But could I go back now to my old way of writing? And was there any point? The approach I had taken before had brought me virtually to a standstill. I had no idea how to put into action what I had come to understand.

I returned home (to Canada) with just over two weeks remaining before the deadline, with my original fifty pages written and a hundred and fifty left to write. I had two choices: write it now, or give it up forever. I made my decision. I would write twelve pages a day, whatever that took. *I wouldn't revise anything* because I didn't have time. It had worked for my students in Africa, and maybe it could work for me.

I started to write what I knew about my subject, and when that was exhausted, I kept on going. Even though I detested what I was writing, I let it unfold however it would. I was following a basic precept of what I would come to call Freefall Writing, even though I had no notion of that at the time.

In those first fifty pages, using an overview of Woolf's writing, I had presented my argument: that she was not just ahead of her time, as most people thought, but so far ahead that she demonstrated in her writing much of what was now considered so revolutionary in post-modern thought. Now, my purpose was to prove what I had said there by showing how these ideas evolved in her work chronologically.

Suddenly, on the fourth day of writing, I had a revelation – an insight so startling and unbidden that it propelled me right out of my chair. The very passages on which I had based my thesis were not post-modern at all. Every one of those unusual patches of writing occurred precisely at moments when Woolf would have had to become aware of herself *as* writing. In other words, far from being driven by an intellectual intention to prove a point about language, she *just didn't want to wake up*. The manoeuvres she went through to avoid that moment became more involved as she got older, until her final breakdown and suicide after dozens of attempts to prove that there *was* no difference between writing and life – that everything had already been written down.

In breaks from writing, I stomped around the snowy streets feeling disorientated and weirdly guilty. "You can't say this!" a part of my mind kept telling me. "Nobody has ever suggested this before – who are you to make this claim?"

And yet I also knew that what I was now saying was true. It was obvious to me that I would never, ever have had this powerful insight if I hadn't started to write this way. A decade of thinking and planning hadn't even brought me close. Yet writing into the teeth of my fear of not knowing how to proceed, and not looking back, had given me access to understanding that lay deeper than my thinking mind could go.

Unfortunately, what I was now saying was also diametrically opposed to what I had said in those first fifty pages. But I had no time to do anything about that now. So I wrote an introduction saying that to give two contrasting viewpoints was what I had intended all along, and submitted the thesis.

Those were scary times in academia. No-one, of course, had ever read my work. A friend had recently submitted his, only to receive an aerogram saying, in effect, "Sorry, this doesn't qualify as a thesis. And don't bother writing back to ask us why not." That my own was in the small percentage that were passed without significant amendments, and that my examiners praised it, came as a huge relief. But it was also confirmation of what I had already experienced as true. As my students in Nigeria had shown me, the way to write, and to learn about writing, was to do it: to start in and not question what came up; to keep on moving forward without looking back.

I felt eager to explore this understanding further. The act of writing the thesis in this way had brought me an important insight, but I had already done years of research on that material. Could writing fiction be trusted in the same way to generate new material that had its own power and integrity? Could I ever write freely enough to find that out?

I cast about for a while, doing freelance editing for several publishers, teaching writing at some local colleges and universities, and writing articles about the Arts. It was striking to me how much of the fiction I was given to edit was well-crafted, but far less complex or interesting than the life being lived all around me, and so much less capable of engaging the heart. A similar ethic seemed to prevail in the institutions where I taught writing. Then a poet of my acquaintance told me about a writing studio at the Banff School of Fine Arts, headed by Canadian novelist W.O. Mitchell, where participants wrote many pages each day. The staff read every page, he said, and gave the writers feedback about what they had done. That sounded like just the kind of approach – and the amount of pressure – I was looking for. I enrolled for the studio.

As early as the second day, it became clear that what I had already learned about writing before I came to Banff had given me a head start. I knew the power of respecting what came up for me, and of not second-guessing myself. I had come here to discover what would happen if I did this, writing creatively. So on the first day of writing, when the sound of tuba players rehearsing in the nearby huts brought a memory of meeting a boy I liked at the bus stop while I was carrying a mellophone, I just went with it – all the way to the music teacher I secretly liked being publicly derided, and how he came to be hounded out of town. I felt utter despair at what I was writing, humiliated as much by the content as by how I wrote. But I had sworn to myself I would not change anything, so I handed it in.

I dragged myself to the next morning's meeting, imagining that they now knew what a mistake it had been to let me into the programme. Then Mitchell started reading aloud – my piece of writing! He had tears in his eyes as he read it out in his mellifluous voice, and I could see that some of the others did, too. Once again it seemed, unbelievably, that following the impulse of the writing into the teeth of this shape-shifter, the fear, and not looking back – not changing anything – had brought me to this moment.

That summer, I discovered the enormous value of autobiography in learning to write spontaneously. Soon I, and many of the others, had mustered much of the abandon my students in Nigeria had found it so easy to achieve. And our writing was complex and absorbing.

I felt eager to begin to teach writing in my own way – one that would allow people to engage deeply with writing *by* writing, and thereby find out the rest of what they needed to know.

Balancing Will and Surrender: The Way a Writer Writes

The cumulative effect of my experiences with writing was a powerful desire to know the answers to three questions. Is it possible to cultivate writing as a truly vulnerable and open-hearted engagement with the moment? Can writing in that way result in something that is of value to a reader? And finally, can this way of writing be taught?

By now, after thirty years of teaching and writing, I know that "Yes" is the answer to all three. And how it works is this. By following what I have called the Freefall Writing precepts, you can quickly learn to become absorbed in the writing, even as your writing (it turns out) becomes absorbing for other people. With repeated experience of writing in this way, you begin to trust that this will happen. And in that state of absorption, you are able to let the writing teach you, because the rational, consciously intending aspect of the psyche (mistakenly often thought of as "the self", but perhaps more properly called "the ego") has stepped out of the way. You can write with an open heart and allow words that you had not planned to write to surface on the page.

From the writing that comes up right away when people begin to follow these precepts, it's immediately evident that the very qualities I used to find missing in the fiction manuscripts I was editing – an aliveness and complexity, a quality of engagement, in short a *believability*, that goes deep enough to make the reader care – are already there. Once a writer has mastered the skill of surrender, he or she can learn to bring some degree of conscious intention back into the process *without* destroying the deep absorption and spontaneity of the writing state – without, if you will, having to break the spell. It's a state into which we can bring conscious thought and intention, *once we have reliably developed the ability to surrender in the first place*.

For example, people who are deeply absorbed in what they're writing quite typically develop the ability to create scenes, write dialogue, or sustain a metaphor – elements of the craft that can be difficult to learn in the abstract – just because that way of doing something occurs to them as the next step, as they write. Once they become aware of what they've accomplished, manoeuvres that were originally unconscious become part of a growing repertoire of technical choices that they are now able *consciously* to employ. This expansion of skills, which even their own writing partner or group, properly instructed, can facilitate, takes place naturally over time. And in this way, people who began to write by using the precepts seem to bypass some of the stages of self-consciousness that can make learning to write in any less hands-on way a kind of agony, forcing many people to stop writing altogether.

What it looks like is this: on any given day, you sit down to write. Early on in the process, you write with no idea of where the writing might lead. Writing without revising, you allow the writing to move in whatever direction has energy and keeps the writing self engaged. After writing for some months, or however long it takes you truly to become accustomed to learning from what that way of writing brings to you, you begin to find yourself capable of bearing in mind some notion of directing the writing, without interrupting the absorption – to "freefall" with more intention. How long it will take to balance the two – to find your own essential balance between will and surrender – you will discover for yourself.

Obviously, there are many writers who have discovered their own internal balance, without recourse to any process such as this. But I think that for many more of us, in our over-thinking culture, the way to reach the parts of us that are hidden has become increasingly difficult to find. And of course, even having found that balance for a period of time is no guarantee of sustaining it. Time and again I find myself working with writers who have written a successful work – a novel, say – and now find themselves lost as to how to proceed. They find themselves lecturing in the next book, or boring people, but why? It seems the ego has taken hold of even that balance as a chance to say, "Now I know what I'm doing!" and with those very words, the ability to surrender is lost. Yet it is possible to find a way of becoming simple again, and of going back, as Yeats put it late in his life, "to the place where all the ladders start": the place he calls "the foul rag and bone shop of the heart".[2]

The exciting thing about this way of writing, with Freefall at the heart of it, is that it is always new, always a process of discovery. You use this process daily, not as an adjunct to your other writing – rather, as the fascinating and sometimes profound exploration that *is* your writing. Freefall puts the ground under your feet as a writer, in a certain sense by taking it away.

Chapter Two
How to Support Yourself as a Writer

Before you begin to engage with the precepts, it's worth taking a little time to consider how you can support yourself in this process – how you can stand by and encourage yourself to write, so that whether you have what you consider to be a bad day or a good one, you'll continue.

I am going to suggest a number of habits that can be of real value to your evolution as a writer, once they are in place. You may already be familiar with or have implemented some of them, and you may already have other habits that you find useful. For the most part, the suggestions I'm about to make are not earth-shattering or revolutionary, but established and developed with care and consciousness as to how *you* feel as you live with them and what works for *you*, they can perform a crucial function in sustaining your writing life.

The Habit of Daily Writing

The very best gift a writer can give him or herself is the habit of sitting down at some point, every day, to write. I wish I could say there was some way around it, because it's not always easy to put another daily activity into our already over-full lives. But for easing your way into the kind of concentration that facilitates writing, there's nothing that helps – nothing whatsoever – like having done it the day before. If you write one day, it's easier the next. As with running or swimming, the process builds on itself. And if you miss a day, the next day's harder. It's as simple as that.

All too often, however, when the writing doesn't go well one day, it's tempting to skip it, the next. Why court discouragement? Why not give yourself a break? At times like this, I find it helpful to remind myself of the way Stephen King describes how he discovered the state in which he writes – a state he thinks of as akin to dreaming awake:

> *I can't remember exactly how I first found that state except that I would sit down to write every day and I would pretty much do that whether the work went well or the work went badly.*[3]

That little phrase, "whether the work went well or the work went badly" serves as a useful mantra to get myself to sit down at the desk.

Fortunately, this habit seems to take amazingly little time to establish. I'm no longer surprised when, deprived of their daily writing time on the last half-day of a week-long workshop, people say "I feel aimless" or "I woke up this morning feeling ready to write!" I'm not surprised, but I do marvel. "One week!" I think. That's how long it took for that habit to form.

Of course, it's easy enough to put the habit of daily writing in place and to maintain it when you're at a workshop, with a deadline and someone encouraging you to write each day. But sheer curiosity is also an excellent motivator. With this way of writing, you truly don't know what's going to happen. If you can let that fact make you curious rather than anxious, the desire to find out will always be there. "I like characters with a reason to get up in the morning," says Peter Temple.[4] And that goes for the writer, too. Not knowing what's going to happen gives *you* a reason to get up in the morning. And to show up, to make sure something does.

I frankly don't think it matters how long you write *for* each day. John Grisham claims that for a long time, his one commitment was to write only one page,[5] but to do that every day. Any amount of writing will keep the portal open, and gives the habit the kind of solidity that's increasingly hard to ignore.

But this isn't about being perfect. It's about creating and maintaining a habit – making space in your life for writing, so the process can continue. So try not to be too hard on yourself if you miss a day. You are still a writer, even if you miss a day. Or two days. Just sit down the next day, and write.

The Habit of Self-Awareness

Writers are always avid for news of the way other writers work: what time of day they write, how often, for how long. That may be because writing is such a lonely profession, we find comfort in knowing there are others who work the way we do. (I, for one, am reassured to know that James Jones said, "After I get up it takes me an hour and a half of fiddling around before I can get up the courage and nerve to go to work."[6]) This curiosity may also be fuelled by recurring hope ("There must be an easier way!"). But no matter what you find out about someone else's writing habits, observing the way *you* write will serve you better than anything else in the long run.

No-one else writes quite the way you do. So start now, observing how you do it. Observe what time of day works best for you. Observe how long you tend to write. Observe the inner critical messages that come up for you as you write. I'll be discussing some ways to make use of those in Chapter Eight. But to do that, you will need to be familiar with them, and by the time you reach that chapter you will already have had plenty of opportunity. Make a note to yourself about what your Inner Critic is saying as you write. Observe too how those messages change.

To record these observations, it's a good idea to keep a writing journal – another file on your computer will do. Although I never look back at the notes I write to myself, just the act of writing them down helps me to remember. Especially at the beginning of a project, I sometimes feel as if I couldn't continue if I didn't tell myself how the writing had gone. It's as if by keeping the journal, I'm accompanying myself. I know that someone cares how it all goes: I do. I observe, and I listen. And over time, I get to know myself as a writer. Then when nothing flows, I can tell myself, "It always goes like this at first." Sometimes I can even feel that little glow in the back of my mind that says, "Things will get better soon."

The Habit of Routine

In the great explorations of the 19th century, one of the (all-male) team members was often designated "Mother", the person the others could rely on to maintain a routine, no matter what conditions they encountered. And in meditation, the aspect of the mind that maintains a cheerful steadiness in the practice is sometimes referred to as "Mother is at home". Writers, no less than explorers and meditators, need to know that whatever happens in their writing, it's being balanced by regular exercise, a peaceful working environment, and a predictable schedule. That way, no matter how far you travel in your writing, your psyche knows it's being cared for: *Mother is at home.*

If you hope to make writing a regular part of your life, know that it helps if the life you live when you're not writing is somewhat predictable too, and in some measure supportive of your writing. Perhaps the most important feature of that predictability, at least during the time before you sit down to write, is quiet. You can find the kind of spaciousness that assists the writing much more easily if you're already feeling settled when you sit down. That's why many people prefer to write in the morning. Certainly, I find that if I have a lunch date, I can't often summon up enough peace of mind to write in the afternoon. It's also noticeably harder to write after I've checked my email, though it's surprising how tenacious that particular habit can be.

I can also feel particularly shell-less after I've been writing. A violent film disturbs me more; everyday worries can feel more burdensome; even a particularly horrifying book can fill me with a kind of despair. See how you feel when you've finished writing. Insofar as it's possible, turn to whatever feels like the most positive alternative, looking out for yourself as you would for a vulnerable (and valuable) friend.

One reliably effective way to handle that thin-skinned feeling is exercise – and in my view it's vital to make that a part of the writing day. Regular, rhythmical exercise, like walking, running or swimming, seems to allow not just the blood, but everything to flow more freely – the writer's thoughts and feelings, too. I can usually tell from the writing when some of the participants at a workshop aren't moving enough: it feels somehow stuck or water-logged emotionally. But when, as is sometimes possible at the residential workshops, there's a whole-group physical exercise option everyone's taking part in, I don't see that kind of stuckness in the writing at all. I've come to think of exercise as allowing energy to circulate through the whole body, whereas with writing, it seems to concentrate in the head.

Yet another good way to support yourself as a writer is to find a regular place to do your writing. I've been dismayed to discover how often, especially among female writers, their writing space is the "guest" room. Of course it seems sensible to make use of an empty room. But unfortunately when guests do come, at the very time when these writers could be setting new boundaries about how available they have to make themselves to guests in their household, they no longer have any familiar place to go and write.

If you can, find somewhere you can leave your basic writing station (a table, a chair) set up, and come back to it each time you write. Even if it's a corner of the attic where you can use your laptop, or (as several male writers I've known with big families have had) your typewriter on a table in the cellar, that little bit of space can be pure gold for a writer. It drains so much less energy to have already "tamed the space", as the Buddhists put it: to know when you get to it, "This is what I do here."

The Habit of Writing on the Computer

Much is talked about the value of writing by hand: the sharpened pencil and the Moleskine notebook; the fountain pen and the lined yellow pad. Of course many writers have their ritual implements, and given how magical good writing can appear to be, it's no wonder we hear in detail about these instruments of sorcery. But there are so many advantages to forming the habit of writing with a computer, I say let's just power them up and do the deed.

One big advantage of writing straight onto the computer is that your work is always legible to you and anyone else – a big advantage, in my case, over writing by hand. Another is that the writing can be filed and therefore found much more easily. When I've later asked people for a particular piece of timed writing that they've read out from their notebooks during a session, a surprising number discover that it can't be found. But if that writing – some of which I will remember all my life – had been done on a computer, or if they had copied it into a file when they got home, I know it would have been much less likely to have been lost (if, that is, you back it up regularly).

The loss of even one piece of writing can turn out to be significant. Playwright John Guare claims that a letter he'd forgotten writing (but which his father had kept) supplied the crucial next step for a play, and as a result, he says, "I realized if I was going to be a writer, I must first trust this unknown work process that goes on within and realize my job as a writer now becomes protecting it."[7] Let the computer help protect it for you. That's a very big part of *its* job.

The computer is also, of course, a major time-saver. If you're a good typist, it will go as fast as you want it to go, and with this way of writing you will sometimes find that the writing does come very quickly. And even if you don't type quickly, you won't have to re-type the work in order to show it to someone else, thus freeing up some time within a schedule that may already have been stretched to its limits by the fact that you're writing at all.

The Habit of Not Talking About Your Writing

Something all writers come to find out quickly is that when they tell people they've been writing, the first question to come back is: "What have you published?" And why not? Curiosity is natural, and the one thing everyone knows about writing is that publishers publish it. But that particular question, though it costs nothing to ask, might very well cost you something to answer in terms of your as yet rather fragile writing self-esteem. So really, why get into it in the first place? Try to form the habit of not talking about your current writing in conversation.

Think of it as a new shoot that needs to be nurtured in the greenhouse, rather than laid bare to the blasts of sun and wind, and every other kind of exposure. And if you do slip up and tell someone that you're writing, you can simply revert, when they ask, to becoming a broken record: "I just said I was writing. And it's going okay." Even if you're not sure it is, you *are* writing, and they will feel reassured.

But what about showing your writing to your family or your friends? When you like what you've just written, and even when you don't, the need to get some feedback can feel strong. The problem I see with doing this is that, given the kind of writing you'll be engaged in, it can be very difficult for most people to know what to say. You're not writing with a plan or an intention, as you'll soon see from the precepts. You're finding out, and learning from, what you do. And that could be any sort of writing at all. I vividly remember a woman I had never met sending me some writing that was so powerful, I could hardly believe my eyes when she went on to say that she had read it out to a group of friends, who had had nothing to say about it. Was it not any good, then, she wanted to know? But when I tried to imagine myself as her friend, listening to this very autobiographical-sounding piece of writing, I found it difficult to think what I might have said. "Can I help you?" (No.) "Do you need therapy?" (She didn't.) "Is this therapy?" (It wasn't.) And even if her friends had managed to say something, it might well have been the old standby, which couldn't be more beside the point: "It didn't happen like that. It happened like *this* …". She'd have had to explain first that it wasn't the content she wanted them to listen for, it was the writing. But the same thing might well have happened, even then.

I don't know of a single writer, anywhere, who doesn't interpret silence in response to his or her work as negative. But the alternative is to ask people to comment on a kind of writing-in-process about which they might well have nothing, or nothing remotely relevant, to say. A friend who is a novelist tells me that she reads the pages she writes each day to her husband that night, and he is allowed to say only one thing: "That's wonderful! Keep going!" It doesn't seem to matter if such a comment has been ritually planned, the ego laps it up anyway. But if that's not the kind of arrangement you'd feel comfortable making, cultivate the habit of not showing your writing to your family or your friends. Consider it an act of mercy to all concerned.

The Habit of Writing With a Partner

As I have said, it feels good – and can sometimes feel imperative – to know that your writing communicates something to another person. So rather than seeking a useful response from people who are unlikely to give you one, consider finding someone with whom you can make it a regular habit to exchange your work. Establish a writing partner, someone who is also writing and can give you feedback that's appropriate to the way you're writing – the kind of response you need to keep your writing on track.

If a partnership like this is not easy for you to find right now, then by all means, just start writing. Many successful writers write for years on their own. But because this kind of writing so often goes beyond what you think you know, the very parts of it you may judge as good don't always turn out to be what's most powerful for another person. And the parts about which you feel most vulnerable or (even more often) self-critical – writing that has in some way taken you to the edge of yourself – can turn out to be what most engages someone else. That's why I find it important, especially early on, to have someone to show your writing to. And very helpful, too, to be able to take in what that person says.

I'll be able to be more specific about the kind of feedback that's most helpful once I've explained the precepts. But in the meantime, here are some practical suggestions.

I believe that you'll find a singular writing partner (or at most, two people) of far more value to you than a larger writing group right now, for a number of reasons. Compared with a group, a pair of writing partners constitutes a very nimble arrangement: you can schedule regular meetings without hours of discussion, and if, alas, one of you hasn't written that week, you can write for an hour together as soon as you meet (using some of the timed writing exercises I give at the end of subsequent chapters, if you like) and then discuss that writing. Even in a relatively short – say, two-hour – meeting, each of you will have ample time to read out your writing and to hear your partner's response. And given the nature of this process, as I've mentioned, it's not helpful to the writer to feel too exposed. For anything I'm writing that's just beginning or still very much in progress, one person's spoken responses to the questions I have posed are all I really need to keep going – and at this stage, keeping going is what I really need to do.

What questions would I pose? Personally, I'd like to know where the energy is for that person in my writing, what's working for them, and why. I need them to be specific. Sometimes I'd like to know what they think the writing is about. If their response sounds flat, or I have any reason to think they might have been bored with what I was reading out, I'd like to know more about that, too. I don't need to know what isn't working for them (experience tells me that, as they say in meditation, "That to which you give energy grows in your life", and that the converse is true, so I want to focus on what *is* working). And I don't remotely need what I think of as copy editing advice: "this sentence is too short", "you've already used this word", and so on. The time for feedback of that sort will come when I have a polished manuscript in hand. Now is the time for exploration, and that kind of information, right now, can only hamper it.

I can take all this information in more deeply if I'm also able to sense physically the responses of the person I'm with. (Did this move them? When did they become thoughtful? Were there times they seemed distracted? Do they mean what they're saying?) For that reason, I strongly prefer meeting with a writing partner face to face, to exchanging work and comments over the internet. In person, I also don't get to assume that they didn't like the writing when in fact they just haven't got around to reading it yet.

If the partnership is to have a good hope of continuing, your writing partner will probably need to value a similar kind of feedback from you about their own writing. But that you can also work through. And if for any reason the partnership has to be dissolved, for the sake of the writing, try to be frank with one another about the reasons. It's never easy, but how much better to admit that you've had no time to write yourself, or are not benefiting from the feedback, or are not by nature drawn to the kind of writing your partner is doing, than to leave that person imagining all that could have been wrong with their writing, or to be left with similar suspicions about your own.

And probably everything I've just said about writing habits has to be balanced by this last one:

The Habit of a "Walk-on Manner"

"And he proceeded in a walk-on manner." That's a refrain that is used frequently by some native North American storytellers, and one I like to use for myself as a writing reminder: "And she proceeded in a walk-on manner." To me, that means moving steadily straight ahead without a lot of drama, and not letting anything bother me very much. Applied to writing, and to any one thing I come to believe I absolutely must have in place in order to do it, that phrase says to me, "Let's not get too precious about all this."

If the writing goes particularly well one day, there's that little voice in the psyche that whispers, "Maybe if I do it *exactly* that way tomorrow, the same thing will happen." But of course, nothing in life stays the same. And just when you've become really attached to a particular habit, that's probably the time to find out what happens if you shake it up a little bit. If you always write in the morning, write at night. If you always write on the computer, write by hand. See what happens. Writing on through the whole continuum of possibilities increases your awareness of yourself as a writer, and will give you that steady, no-nonsense, long-distance attitude to writing that constitutes a "walk-on manner".

Tha Habit of Letting Habits Develop Themselves

There's a risk that talking about any of these useful writing habits in advance is putting things the wrong way around. Habits or rituals that work tend to develop along the way, as a result of your having started to do something you value, not work because they've already been put in place.

Anyone who has taken long walks, for days or weeks at a time, will recognise this phenomenon: when you've already been walking for several days, especially with other people, you start to notice a spontaneous ritual emerging around what I think of as "the tying of the boot". When it's time to lace their boots up in the morning, everyone starts to become a little quiet. The swellings, the blisters and tenderness you're all starting to feel – and the growing importance to all of you by now of not wanting to *stop* walking – means that this particular moment of the walk has begun to feel more pivotal. You want to put a blister plaster down in here, and tighten this part, but maybe if you just left this part a little looser... Everyone stops talking at once because they're all thinking the same sort of thing.

But it's because you've already walked quite a distance that this ritual has arisen. It's good to have good boots in the first place, and to have brought some plasters along with you. But whatever else you might have anticipated needing, you may well have had to jettison along the way. The journey itself has given this way of doing things importance. Once writing has become as important to you as walking has in this situation, you'll start to attend to what supports it in your own unique way.

Right now, it's time to start walking: to summon the courage and the faith to begin at the beginning, to put aside skills and beliefs, and even good plans for useful writing habits and – to paraphrase Theodore Roethke – to learn by going where you have to go.[8] In the precepts I will outline in the next chapter, you'll find the help you need to do just that.

Chapter Three
The Five Precepts

Over the years, I've developed some simple guidelines to make the process of surrender in writing easier and faster. The five most important of these, jokingly called "the Five Precepts" by some, are easily stated. They never seem to change, although my understanding of them continues to evolve and my current take on them shifts constantly. I suggest that you take these suggestions to heart but hold them lightly, much as you would a meditation technique, like "follow the breath". Keep coming back to them. Over time, they will both further and renew your exploration.

Here are the precepts. I will state all five briefly, then explore each of them a little more fully.

1. Write what comes up for you
Begin to write, without any particular plan in mind of what you are about to say. Start anywhere. Then, whatever occurs to you once you have started writing, write it down. "It has one justification," as poet William Stafford says of his own very similar practice, "It occurs to me."[9]

2. Don't change anything

Whatever it is you've written, leave it on the page (or screen) just as it is. Don't change it. Simple? It *is* simple. But this is the precept most writers seem to find hardest to follow.

3. Give all the sensuous detail

Wherever you may find yourself, don't forget to say how things feel, look, taste and smell, and what can be heard there. Give specific, sensuous detail.

4. Go where the energy is, or go fearward

As you write, be aware of moving toward whatever feels most charged to you. If several things come up at once, choose the one that strikes you the most forcefully, whether you're attracted or repelled. And if you're still not sure, choose the one you're most afraid to write about. Go fearward.

5. The Ten-Year Rule

If what comes up for you is autobiographical, know that if it's more than ten years old, it will be more resonant than will recent material, and easier to work with. It will, to use Natalie Goldberg's word, have "composted".[10]

Bear in mind that your goal is to follow all five precepts at the same time. Doing so takes a little practice, and for a while you'll probably find yourself remembering one to the exclusion of the others as you write. This slightly awkward stage reminds me of learning to ride a bicycle: too much sensuous detail and you tip over to one side. Too much going fearward and you tip over to the other. But when the amount of sensuous detail is balanced by content that grips you, you'll stay steady and shoot forward, effortlessly and smoothly.

Notice that I *don't* say, "Keep writing as fast as you can" or "Don't stop moving your fingers on the keyboard". Usually called "freewriting" or "free association", that technique is intended, I think, to get you moving ahead so quickly that you'll surprise yourself by outstripping your usual way of doing things. The stream-of-consciousness style of writing that usually results from writing very quickly, or writing without stopping, tends to stay on one level emotionally, expressing whatever arises from moment to moment in consciousness, but never taking the writer away from the current moment in the way that following all five precepts will.

While the first two guidelines or precepts might be taken as "freewriting" instructions, when you add in the other three, the writing takes on a different character entirely. When you're "going where the energy is" for you, "giving all the sensuous details" of what you find there, and following "the ten-year rule", you're entering a world that's different from the one you currently inhabit. It's only natural to pause, look more closely, and write again as you find your way.

But remember: writing in this way, meditatively and with pauses, is one thing; getting up to answer the phone or see what's in the refrigerator is another.

Now that I have introduced you to the five guidelines that I believe are most important, let's spend a little more time with each of them to see in more detail what they mean and how they work.

Writing What Comes Up for You

They appear off the end of the pen, at that wondrous point of connection and delight, and place themselves freely in my drawings. They ask for things and do what they will.

- Michael Leunig

To better understand what's meant by this precept, it may be useful to begin by understanding what it *doesn't* mean. It doesn't mean thinking about what you're going to write before you start. It doesn't mean beginning with a plan. It doesn't mean beginning on the writing project you've always dreamed of undertaking. It may be precisely that dream project that's been keeping you from writing in the first place. If a subject truly has energy for you, then it will come up one of these days in the course of writing. But in the meantime, there may be other things that need to be written first, and you won't discover what those are unless you let yourself remain truly free.

A few years ago, a young man in one of my workshops admitted on the introductory go-round that he wanted to write a novel that dealt with the relationship between a Muslim man and a Christian woman and their families (he was Muslim himself), a love story perhaps, and to write it in such a way that people who read it would empathise with both points of view and understand both cultures better. He thought it could help with what was going on in England at the time. But he'd had trouble getting started. As I listened to him, I wondered to myself how anyone *could* get started on a novel with such a heavy burden of responsibility resting on his shoulders. Perhaps his is an extreme example (to me, it was also a very touching one), but a surprising number of us come to writing with similarly well intentioned but self-inhibiting schemes.

Now is the time to set those notions aside and just start writing. Start with anything at all. "It is like fishing," as William Stafford observes.[11] And a fish will come. The line will jerk, perhaps almost imperceptibly, and you'll be off, following the pull of something that has energy for you. Stay with whatever that is until the energy moves away again.

People often ask me whether it's all right to come back to a subject or a story they started but don't feel finished with from the previous day's writing. I'd say yes, *if* it still has energy for you – if your mind goes spontaneously to it. But don't grab that story like a lifeline to avoid the uncertainty of not knowing where the writing will take you. That sense of not knowing will always be waiting for you, and this is your chance to become more accustomed to it, rather than hope it will go away, or let it put you off writing altogether.

Please remember, too, that as I said, that moment of connection with a subject, that tug on the line, may be almost imperceptible. Many of us come to writing with the illusion – the legacy, I think, of the Romantic poets – that when we're on the right track, we will feel truly inspired. We'll be found on some rocky pinnacle like an Art Nouveau maiden, lost in a trance with the wind of divine *afflatus* whipping our muslin dress around our thighs. Alas, that sense of rightness and conviction, when it comes at all, tends to be fleeting. More often, there's just a hunch, an image, a rhythm, or even a tone of voice that signals the connection: a small shift from nothing to something. At times no direction is discernible at all, and the important thing is just to keep writing, with the trust that something will come. Sometimes "one gropes about in misery for a while," as Virginia Woolf noted on her way to *The Waves*.

Not Changing Anything

Just as lethal to the writing state as getting up to answer the phone or gaze into the refrigerator is second-guessing yourself. Instead, leave what you've written on the page and keep going. Someday, you can go back and change it, if it still looks like it needs to be changed. For now, your job is to write.

Another way of understanding this precept is to realise that, for now, you need to remain *the writer*. When you shift into the mode of reading back and changing things, you change gears and become, instead, the reader. The reader in you is already strong from years and years of practice, at school and ever since. It's not going to weaken or die from underwork, and it doesn't need to sharpen its skills in this moment, either. What needs to be developed and strengthened in you right now is the writer, and the writer's job is simply to write.

It always surprises me, although by now it shouldn't, how often the first version of something works best. When I read someone's hand-written work and can see the places where she or he has changed a word or a phrase, I find more often than not that it worked better the first time. The interpolated word or phrase is slightly out of context, or at a different level of diction, or just generally out of tone with the rest of the writing, so that it stands out and draws a little too much attention to itself. What came in the thick of the original movement forward had *the virtue of being a product of its time*, even if a word was repeated, or three words did the work of one. So for now, just stay with what comes up for you (including typing errors) and don't read back. When you've left it for long enough that you've forgotten about it, what you've said will often look inevitable. If not, there will be plenty of time at that stage to make changes.

A word on spelling. There are people who almost can't bear to leave a spelling mistake on the page. Nonetheless, I suggest you leave it alone. Correcting the spelling involves the same sort of shift from writer to reader, from creator to critic, that I've been talking about, and is therefore a good thing to avoid. I used to feel embarrassed about misspellings. Would people think I was ignorant? That I didn't know "their" from "there"? Then one day I heard Margaret Atwood's mother being interviewed on the radio. She was talking about what a terrible speller "Peggy" had been at school. "She spelled words phonetically," she said admiringly. "She wasn't seeing them, you see, she was listening to a voice." Hearing her say that made it much easier for me to leave spelling errors on the page. "I'm listening to a voice," I'd tell myself. Who knows? It might even be true.

When I began to teach writing, people were still using typewriters. The typewriter would print the words and hold them fast on the page. Now, computers make it all too easy to change things; indeed, it seems to be integral to using the computer that we correct what we've just written, almost without thinking. In that sense, it's a monument to our dysfunction. Because of this almost automatic correcting, I often recommend covering or turning off the screen. I won't forget a photograph one of my students showed me of her writing group on Rottnest Island in Western Australia, one of them at a keyboard with a large green bundle in front of her that was bigger than her head. "What's that thing in front of Nicola-Jane?" I asked, and she looked at me as if the answer was obvious: "Her monitor, with a blanket over it." Repeatedly, people tell me that they've finally tried turning off the screen and it's made all the difference. But don't forget to look down at the keyboard to see where your fingers are, once in a while. And don't forget to save.

Specific, Sensuous Detail

Much could be written, and will be in the course of this book, about the value of specific, sensuous detail. What you need to know from the outset is this: it's important to sense the world you're writing about with your whole body. Slow down and open into it as you write. Stay alive in your senses and aware of what they bring to you.

"Sensuous" is just the right word for this sort of detail:[12] "sensory" is dry and clinical, but with "sensuous" you can almost feel your skin tingling as the breath passes over it. It's immediately evocative, and that's what sensuous details do: they evoke.

And yet they also seem to do much more than just evoke. I often think that sensuous details must act to take us into a different part of the brain – perhaps into the right side of the brain we've heard so much about. But the fact is that when we pay attention to the sensuous details as we're writing, unexpected things happen. They generate new associations. Memories seem to arise that we had forgotten. The world we're writing about opens up in a new way, and allows us to come closer.[13]

When I read people's writing, in addition to letting them know where the energy is for me in the writing, I use "<" or " >", an "open out" mark, to indicate where I think it would be good to have more specific, sensuous, detail. Often the mark points to something the writer didn't think it was necessary to go into. It's easy to forget, when you're in the midst of a world yourself, that there's someone along with you who also needs to know what's being experienced there. Or it may be a place the writer is hurrying by to get to somewhere more important, somewhere he or she considers to be "the point". But frankly, that point won't seem worth getting to if we haven't really participated in the journey along the way. It may even be that the writer simply doesn't know how much sensuous detail is needed in order for someone else to share the experience. But for now, overdo it if you must. Give *all* the sensuous details. They'll bring things to you that you might never have consciously anticipated.

And just as you would remind yourself to register a specific taste, a smell, a sound, or a touch, remember too to use direct speech (I said, "Don't touch me today, Arthur") rather than reported speech (I told Arthur not to touch me today) when it comes up. Dialogue too is a specific, sensuous detail – something that can be heard directly with the ear of the mind.

In a sense, what this surrendered, Freefall Writing is all about is learning to become absorbed in what you're writing. And I don't know of any quicker way to do that than through paying attention to specific, sensuous detail.

Following the Energy

Well, except one.

The very best way to learn how to become absorbed in your writing is to write about something that grips you. What could make better sense, really, than to write about the things that have a charge for you when they come up, as they come up, regardless of what the thinking, reflecting mind has to say about it. Yet all too often, especially when someone is new to writing, the emergence of a subject that the writer finds truly energising provokes a hasty retreat. "If it stirs me up like this," is the thinking mind's reaction, "I'd better write about something else." My strong suggestion is that instead of dismissing a subject that has energy when it emerges, you turn toward it. The experience of writing that it has to offer you will prove invaluable.

After a while, you will become adept at discerning what has energy for you and what doesn't. But as long as that distinction isn't entirely clear, I say "Go fearward". Check with yourself to see if there might be something you're avoiding writing about. It may even have popped up recently – such subjects have a way of doing that – and been dismissed again. And whatever it is that fills you with a desire for avoidance ("Oh no, not that one. Anything but that."), write that. Such a subject will assure you of the kind of edge that makes for excellent writing, if you can stay with it.

Robert Burdette Sweet, in a book called *Writing Towards Wisdom: The Writer as Shaman*, says a similar thing in a more manly fashion: "Best we feel very sweaty about our subjects."[14] Sweet's thesis is that sweatiness has to do with an obsession, and that obsession usually has to do with a taboo. And since "literature is drama, and the greatest tension comes from the expression of a taboo, we should not be surprised to realize that *Oedipus* explores incest, *Medea* infanticide, *Crime and Punishment* murder for its own sake,"[15] and so on. He even suggests that writers "make a list of cultural taboos, find one that personally makes you sweat the most"[16] and then write about that. From my own observation, a far more organic way for a writer to experience the sort of tension Sweet has in mind is simply not to *avoid* such subjects when they come up to be written about. Because they will come up. That's why we call them obsessions.

Whatever way you choose to think about it, working fearward assures you of the experience of absorption in your writing, at the same time as it serves to expand the scope of what you're willing to write about. In fact, in terms of scope, it may not matter as much what you write about as that you don't *prevent* yourself from writing about anything. In addition to all its other virtues, the repeated experience of going fearward fosters the kind of openness to the moment, whatever comes up, that is virtually a pre-requisite to the creative act, as well a prime condition for its continuance.

Waiting Ten Years

When what comes up when you sit down to write is autobiographical, this precept comes into play – and it is to be held as a suggestion, rather than as a hard and fast rule: older material works better, and will teach you more. Obviously, if there's some recent event or impression in the forefront of your consciousness that keeps coming up and just won't go away, you'll need to give it attention in your writing, if only to get it out of the way. And the fact is that people often turn in pieces of writing based on recent material that work wonderfully and are a pleasure to read.

But more frequently, when the material is less than ten years old, I'll find myself thinking as I read, "Why can't I get into this? It's as if there's someone standing in front of me, blocking my way." After a few wrong guesses about why that could be happening, I'll realise, "Aha! This must be recent material. They're still too invested in trying to make sure we'll see it their way." That degree of ego-involvement often manifests in an over-active narrator who feels almost like a traffic policeman, saying no, no, go this way, and pointing with a large, white-gloved hand.

By contrast, material from ten years ago or more tends to have the quality of a world sufficient unto itself, untouched by the concerns of the present day. While we can enter it as a writer and show what's there, we're in a very different state of mind from the one in which we approach more recent material – more willing to witness and less eager to intervene. The specific details of that world, whether remembered or

35

invented, feel resonant and connective. It's become what Virginia Woolf calls "a globed, compacted thing, over which thought lingers and love plays". *This state of mind is invaluable to a writer.* Don't deprive yourself of it. Remember this precept.

What Freefall Writing Is Not

What the writing will turn out to be for you, when you write bearing all five of these guidelines in mind, you won't know until you act on the Writing Experience suggestions at the end of this chapter. But even before you start, it may be a good idea to remind yourself, once again, that what you are undertaking in this writing is an apprenticeship in surrender – a way (in fact, the only way I know) to learn to get out of your own way in writing, and to find out what happens when you do.

Ultimately, once you have mastered that skill, you will be able to use it in the service of whatever you want your writing to accomplish. Right now, your job is simply to follow the precepts. Think of this writing as practice, if that helps you to relax your intention: a practice that will in time become a permanent feature of whatever kind of writing you choose to do.

Before they've begun to write in this way, people sometimes ask me if it will be like journaling, or "morning pages",[17] or Natalie Goldberg's "writing practice".[18] The short answer to all three questions is "No"; the long answer: "Try it first, and see." But a concept that may be helpful in picturing the difference is this: think of writing as a continuum, stretching from "telling" (summarising or even just referring to) events at one end, to "showing" them (recounting them in full sensuous detail) at the other. Journaling and "morning pages" tend to fall at the "telling" end: you simply refer to people or events in the writing because you already know what you're talking about. "Writing practice", which Goldberg sees as "turn[ing] over and over the organic details of your life",[19] amounts to a more opened up form of journaling, falling somewhere around the middle. But as you continue to follow the five precepts, the writing falls closer and closer to the "showing" end of the continuum, moving steadily deeper into the imaginative process.

36

The other big difference from "writing practice" is, of course, that writing in this way is part of a process. Following the precepts into full familiarity with surrender in writing, you can then begin to bring in intention, a little at a time, until you are using the skills you have learned via the precepts, within a genre. Writers frequently come to me saying they have chests full of "writing practice", and no idea what to do with them. But when you write according to the precepts, deepening their use in the ways I suggest in these chapters, your writing will evolve to the point at which, ultimately, you will be able to direct it in any fashion you choose.

Writing On Your Own

At the end of each chapter from here on, I will give you suggestions for Freefall Writing and timed writing exercises to do on your own. Each set of suggestions for this Writing Experience comes with a brief, explanatory preface relating it to the content of the chapter.

In the beginning, I suggest you set aside an hour a day to do the suggested Freefall Writing, and – for the days when you can't do that, or are writing with a partner – use the timed writing topics to do a shorter piece of writing, so that you keep your hand in. Timed writing is quicker and some would say "easier" because you're given a topic, but Freefall Writing asks you to search within and begin to establish your own authority in finding your subject or subjects – ultimately a much more necessary skill.

A reminder: if you write the timed writing exercises by hand while you're away from your computer, don't forget to enter them into a file on your computer when you get home.

Writing Experience

FREEFALL WRITING

Following the five precepts, write what comes up for you for at least an hour every day. Go where the energy is for you, and don't change anything. Remember to open out into all the sensuous details.

Share the piece that has the most energy for you with your writing partner, if you have one. If not, just go ahead and write another one. After all, alone is how you'll end up writing someday. Readers will come along, but in the meantime, here's a chance to get used to it.

Writing Tip: I consider "I don't remember" to be an editorial comment.[20] Don't bother saying that. Just go ahead and write whatever's there.

TIMED WRITING

These are exercises you can do alone, with a timer, or with your writing partner. Let the topic suggest to you a place to begin, and write for ten minutes. Then, if you are with a partner, read out what you've written.

1. A sound heard in childhood (This topic, taken from Peter Elbow's *Writing Without Teachers*, starts you off with a sensuous detail. You can think up others that do the same, such as:)
2. I'll never forget that smell
3. Hearing my name in the night
4. "Talk to me like the rain, and let me listen" (the title of a one-act play by Tennessee Williams)
5. A slap
6. Nothing has ever tasted so sweet
7. Don't go near the water
8. Homesick (or: Home, sick)

Writing Tip: Let the topic take you into a specific incident or scene. Don't stay above it, musing "about" the topic.

Chapter Four
Let One Thing Lead to Another

Now that you've had some experience following the precepts, it may be a good time to explore their implications a little more deeply, starting with the first guideline, "Write what comes up for you", and the third, which is closely linked to it: "Give all the sensuous detail". It's important to be clear about some of their implications, because what they actually require of you is subtle but far-reaching.

Writing What Comes Up

After people have begun to write in this surrendered, Freefall way, a curious phenomenon often occurs: a cascade of "things to write about" seems to begin in the brain. "So many things came to me last night," writers often tell me on the second day of a workshop, "I've made a list of topics I want to write about." Glad as I am that they're so eager to keep writing, I can't help noticing that what they now suddenly want to do directly contravenes the first precept of the way they've just been writing: *Write what comes up.* That means, as I've explained to them, *don't* plan and *don't* have topics. But I can understand their wanting to. The very act of writing without a plan seems to activate some mad planning genie in the brain, causing ever more brilliant ideas for writing to rise up unbidden.

Analyse this paradox though I may, I keep coming to the same conclusion: there is something threatening to what I have called the "intending" self, or ego, about stepping off into the unknown in writing. Anything could happen. What will happen is beyond the ego's control.

That state of uncertainty is by definition uncomfortable. It can be deeply uncomfortable. To stay in that state requires what some spiritual teachers call "intentional suffering" – willing oneself to stay in a situation that's causing discomfort, for the sake of a greater good that can be brought about that way. Yet that is exactly what the day to day life of a writer – or anyone who wants to stay open to the larger knowing available to them – requires. ("I follow what I see on the paper in front of me – one sentence after another," as Harold Pinter noted.[21])

To put it a different way, what the powerful urge to plan (and thereby avoid uncertainty) doesn't take into account is the fact that if we let ourselves truly risk not knowing, something new can happen that might never happen any other way. And for anyone who really commits him- or herself to a life of creativity, that degree of risk-taking is the daily routine.

Helena McEwen has evoked its trajectory superbly with reference to painting in the following timed writing piece. (Please note that here, as with all the Freefall Writing quoted in this book, the writing is unedited and appears exactly as it was spontaneously written.)

Blank. I keep going into my studio but I don't know why. I feel terrified of this unknown, because of "people working alone, and undisturbed by the outside world", oh goodness, if only there WAS a disturbance. If only there was a human being in the next room, someone who'd disturb me and say, "Oh, want a cup of tea?" Even a dog. It's when you're in there, okay then, when I am, and something drags you in, beyond, beyond the place you know. Be there, this is hard, the canvas is going somewhere I don't like. We started off okay. It was a gentle place to be, fun. There was pink in there, the colours of light, magenta, and orange, and some cool blue grey. But something opened. Not yet, we were in there, in that space of colour, trying to bring it to earth, trying to join them together, so the heart dances and sings and opens wide in joy. It can be done. But then that red, it didn't mix properly and it's yellow red, terrifying, cutting like a gash through the gentleness, reminding me of, itself, a wound endless and unhealed. I try to bring it back, to scrub it out, but it refuses. "I am here, know me, accept me, I am your deepest pain." Does it seem mad? And then I am lost, being hurtled into some terrifying blood red space, that old place, some ancient massacre, bodies torn, yellow wigwams and black smoke. Remember, remember. The space sucks me into a place of terror and pain. I can't find my way out, it won't let me go. The picture is out of control, colours of mud and black, chaos, it is my within place, it sneers at me, it is ugly, it is my ugliness. I stop and pray. There are four who help. The one who comes is blue. She is compassion. She steps into the painting delicately. She steps in through violet. A red violet that soothes my terrified red. A cobalt violet that lightens the mud, and a gentle lilac that brings back air. Before long some lemon yellow is dancing along the black stripes, and bright pink returns and makes me smile with relief. It's okay, it's okay, it's gone through its death and chaos, I fell apart there for a bit, got torn to pieces, but it's come out the other side and I'm whole again. There we are now. Make a cup of tea!

One of many things worth noticing in this piece of writing is that the arc of discovery as McEwen describes it here takes place entirely *as a result of the activity* of painting. The artist doesn't come to the canvas with a plan, nor does she paint toward some pre-set goal she has in mind. She begins to paint, and the whole journey evolves from that activity. "Begin to write," says the description of the first precept in the previous chapter, and follow what occurs to you. First, begin to write. *Thinking simply doesn't work in the same way writing does.*

What's also abundantly clear for the painter in McEwen's piece is that there are no guarantees. That's part of what's implied by the word "uncertainty". There's the risk that the painting may go nowhere. It may be ruined. It may reach into what she calls "my within place", the somewhere "endless and unhealed" that the ego fears will prove to be unbearable. If we are to be – as the artist in her piece is committed to being – fully available in the moment, then everything we hold onto must be surrendered. We don't get to keep certain things back, and choose to use others. Why then do we do it? I've always liked the succinctness with which Australian novelist Drusilla Modjeska answers that fundamental question: "I'd prefer to run the risks than stultify, not having lived life fully."[22] Surprisingly often in the process of writing, one discovers that that really does seem to be the choice.

But the act of writing doesn't just lead you into a place of unknowing and leave you there. Like the painter in the piece you've just read, you are engaged in an activity when you write that has its own logic and its own ways of proceeding. *That* path is the one that's available for you to follow now, rather than the straitened track of your pre-conceived intentions.

Perhaps you can recall the way in which, when you had learned to write essays following a pre-conceived outline, the writing would keep marching off in its own direction, forcing you to drag it back in manacles to the outline once again? What you're being asked to do now is to follow the writing, and discover where *it* wants to lead you – for a paragraph, or two, or even for the whole of the journey.

Specific, Sensuous Detail

The good news about this demanding and unpredictable process is that as a writer, you are never entirely alone in it. Just as a painter relies on paints to find a way forward, so you can depend on the power of sensuous detail. If you can allow yourself to stay fully present to those details in the writing, then surprisingly often, one thing *will* lead to another and, with trust, you will find your way.

Staying in the immediacy of specific, sensuous detail, however, is not always easy – and especially not at first. If the material that is emerging in the writing comes from your past, you may find that it's only possible to remain with those details for moments at a time before backing away. The image that often comes to me when I read people's first attempts at this kind of writing is of someone repeatedly putting a hand in the fire and pulling it out again as it gets too hot. With practice, the length of time one *can* stay present for those details increases steadily. And with the ability to stay present for them, a surprising number of other capacities unfold: authority; a steady voice; a sense of direction, of rhythm and timing, and at times of humour; and the power to bring about an appropriate ending – all of which seem to become possible because of that sustained connection with the sensuous detail.

Take a look, by way of example, at this piece of writing by Mary Hancock, in which the tension between the desire to back away from powerful sensuous detail and the will to stay present gives rise to an unexpected central figure with a life of its own. (Just how early on in the process it was created can be inferred from the topic, my first-day favourite: "A Sound Heard in Childhood".)

Slap, yelling, anger, the sound of my younger brother banging his head against the wall at the end of the bed, the sound of my mother pummelling my brother and saying it would have been better if you'd died when you were a baby, the slap of a beaver's tail on the water makes me think of Wind in the Willows, stuff and bother, I hate spring cleaning, freedom, a beaver slaps its tail on the water to warn of people coming. A beaver escapes into its house and hides. Darkness. But it is safe in there. It can swim easily under water; it doesn't have to worry about what to be when he grows up. Slap. The sound of a hand hitting my head. The sting on my cheek. The blood that rushes to my face. The shame that floods me ... keep writing, keep writing ... we never went camping, but I think I read about beavers in my social studies book; the industrious beaver, finding twigs to make a home in the river. I'd look at the picture and feel the water, gliding through it like vaseline – maybe I think it was like that because of the cold I didn't feel – my fur keeps the coldness from me. And I know how to swim and how to build this house where it is safe. Of course, it isn't really like that, there isn't a magical world where animals talk, and live in cosy burrows, and have adventures along the river bank; my sharp teeth biting through the bark, which tastes sweet and tangy at the same time, gnawing away, slap of the tail on the water warning of danger, hide until the people go away. It's dark under the water but I like it like that. I like to be able to go to places that people don't go. The mud at the bottom holds no fear for me. I nose around there looking for small fish that sleep there during the day. Sometimes I float on my back on top of the water, looking at the sky, scudded with clouds. Still listening for the sound of danger. It was a thrill the first time I slapped my tail on the water loud enough to warn of danger. My tail is a perfect design. My fur keeps me warm. I can live under water and breathe air. I do what I do very well. My house meets my needs; I built it myself. I am self-sufficient.

At first, it's striking how clearly one can hear the different impulses or voices within the author (or, to be more accurate, the narrator), pulling in their various directions. Immediately comes the one who is present to the sensuous details: the sounds of the slap, the banging, the angry words, the pummelling. Then comes impulse to turn away – to that same sound when it's made by the beaver, and to another of childhood's routes of escape: the imagination, *The Wind in the Willows*. Again the hand is thrust back into the fire – the slap again, on the I-character's own face this time, the visceral assault of it, quickly followed by the impulse to pull away entirely (countered by "keep writing, keep writing"). At this point, the critical impulse makes its presence felt: but what did I know about beavers? "We never went camping." And "of course [...] there isn't a magical world where animals talk." But even as that voice starts chiding, the narrator moves steadily further into sensuous detail – now of the beaver *as* the I-character, "gliding through the water like vaseline [...] my sharp teeth biting through the bark, which tastes sweet and tangy." As all the voices settle into that one forward impulse, the piece finds its way smoothly to an apt conclusion (made poignant by its contrast with all that has gone before): the beaver at peace in a safe house of its own making, alone and self-sufficient, with no-one else anywhere in sight.

Metaphor, a figure of speech that works by substitution, is also called a "trope" in literary criticism, and one meaning of trope is "a turning". Reading this piece, I seem to be seeing the anatomy of metaphor: it traces the whole movement by which consciousness turns away and invokes a substitution. This is a perfect evocation, to me, of that sacred act of turning.

Over and over in this kind of writing, I see writers find their way *through blind faith in sensuous detail* – so often that it would be impossible for me not to share that faith. At times, as with the piece we have just read, the writing is sufficiently transparent to let that process show.

In a workshop setting, participants hear a good deal of such writing early on, which in turn prompts them to make the decision to adopt that faith. So I think it would be worthwhile to give you another example. The piece that follows, by Sandy MacDonald, was also written on the first day of a workshop – not as a timed exercise, but with the usual injunctions to go fearward, not to change anything, and to remember the sensuous detail. Though long, it is worth quoting in its entirety, because it shows so clearly how a variety of intellectual impulses (motivated, I think, by fear) cut in to short-circuit the writing, while simply concentrating on sensuous detail *brings the writer further and further into the story.*

When I was four I lost a couple of friends by drowning, but I don't have much to say about it. They were Jackie and Blair. One was a girl and one was a boy and I can't remember which was which, I wasn't present at the scene of the drowning. I might have been there. They had to pass my yard to go down to the pond where they died. I seem to remember them going by, asking me, as I stood in my grassy front yard under the purple sycamore tree, lost in some play, asking me if I wanted to go down to the pond with them. There was a steep bank down from my yard into a ditch and then the dirt road, sloping down from Green Hill into the woods. I see them standing in the dust of the road and talking to me. I didn't go over to talk to them. I stayed in the grass where I had been playing, but I looked toward them. They were older than I was by a year or two, but I played with the girl sometimes. It was summer. We were all children let out to play for the afternoon. I didn't go with them. I don't even know now if that image I have is a memory or an invention. I imagine they gave me the choice to go with them, since they had to pass by so close, and since I sometimes played with Jackie, the girl. Maybe they didn't ask. Maybe I saw them pass and not invite me. I do remember going with my mother to Jackie's house. Our mothers were good friends. My mother went to be with her friend in grief. I wish she hadn't taken me. Although I was sad, I couldn't be part of the scene of grief. Jackie's mother was lying on her bed, sobbing. My mother was sitting on the bed beside her. It was a little room and I wished I could get some more distance between myself and the emotion of these mothers.

They say that drowning is, after a certain stage, a euphoric experience. My friends found a raft on the shore of the pond. That was nothing unusual, I have found rafts there myself. The pond is at the Atlantic shore. It is separated from the Atlantic by a sand bar, a beach. It is a completely dead pond. It was the big pond, maybe Big Pond. At one end was the Atlantic and at the other end was a coal mine. The coal mine pumped its waste water into Big Pond. Whatever was in that waste turned the pond copper. It turned all the rocks and beach along the shore of the pond copper. Yet children loved to go and play there, and apparently people loved to go rafting there because we all used to find these rafts. They would be driftwood logs somehow nailed together, all turned copper from being left in the pond. There was no seaweed along its shore, or in the shallows. The pebbles along its shore were perfectly free of that slimy growth you often find on wet stones at the edge of the water. I guess it was the calm of the water that drew people to it. Unlike the ocean just over there, Big Pond had no waves to speak of. It was perfect for rafting, if all you wanted was to get out onto the water. Get a pole and push off from the shore, maybe use a board as a paddle when the pole couldn't reach the bottom. Or maybe just trust to luck and the wind to bring you back to the ground. It is a beautiful thing to be on the water, maybe with your legs over the side, splashing in the coppery brown water, floating, drifting. The summer sun would be glaring and flashing in the ripples from your legs and feet. The flashes are hot, the water is cool. The driftwood logs are smooth and uneven and warm. They took their clothes off. They were found naked. They stood there for a moment on their raft in the glare and heat of the sun shining off the coppery water. All around was this darkness of water with a shiny surface. They must have looked at each other in the bright light, though they were children, a girl and a boy. The breeze wasn't taking them back down to the shore. There was no breeze. After a while they would start to worry, when they thought again of time and mothers and getting home for supper. In their worry they decided on a plan to swim, to jump and try their strength and skill against the cool brown water with its shining skin so fragile and so thin. So down they jumped and it hurts my chest to go with them now into the cool brown darkness. I don't want that feeling of failing strength and failing skill, the loss of breath precious delicious breath. People who have been rescued from drowning at the last moments say there is a turning. They say, whether it is a memory or an invention who can say, but they say the sounds that come through the water make a music, and there is a feeling of perfect freedom in the floating and the light coming through the water is more purely beautiful than anything.

At times in the piece it seems as if *only* staying with the sensuous detail makes writing this bearable for the writer, and yet the narrative moves steadily closer in to Jackie and Blair's story: from don't know, to would be, to must have been, to was. It's a long way from "I lost a couple of friends by drowning, but I don't have much to say about it," to the deep and painful intimacy that's finally forged with these children, just as it's a long way from "I wasn't present at the drowning," to "it hurts my chest to go with them now into the cool brown darkness." Yet the sensuous details make that growing presence possible. We move from one to the next like stepping stones, not drowning but checking in, yes, still breathing, until at the last we can even hear their music. And it's wonderful to hear the narrative voice find its own ring and rhythm along the way.

Even with an experienced writer like Helena McEwen, it's possible to see how she refocuses *to stay present to the sensuous details,* each time the narrative threatens to pull away. "It's when you're in there, okay then, when I am," she reminds herself in the piece quoted earlier in the chapter, "be there, this is hard" and then, "There was pink in there, the colours of light, magenta, and orange, and some cool blue grey." "Not yet," the narrator tells herself again, when she's tempted to rush on. The urge to move away from whatever constitutes "fearward" never really leaves us, so such reminders become habitual for anyone who writes this way. Like MacDonald, she moves steadily from the general to the particular, from "telling" *about* what happens "when you're in there, okay then, when I am, and something drags you in, beyond, beyond the place you know," to "showing" that experience *as* it happens, right on the page with the colours, moment by moment. We'll come back to that "showing/telling" distinction in the next chapter. Your task right now is simply to remember this: stay with the sensuous details, and you will find your way.

Absorbing or Self-Absorbed?

"What makes the difference between boringly self-centred and interestingly personal?" one writing student has asked me. While her interest in the question stems, I think, from the fact that she is writing a memoir, the answer to that question certainly also pertains to this way of writing as a process. In my experience, one hallmark of writing that strikes me as self-absorbed, rather than (to use my own vocabulary) available to me as a reader, is precisely the *absence* of specific, sensuous detail.

One thing that can happen when autobiographical material emerges in the writing is that the writer steps out of the witnessing stance that makes that world available in writing, and into a more analytic position. "I can see now that the drama of my friends' drowning has affected my life in many ways," Sandy MacDonald might have written, for example, and gone on to elaborate. Or, when "some ancient massacre, bodies torn, yellow wigwams and black smoke" came up in Helena McEwen's piece, she might (to give another example) have continued, "Do I really believe in past lives? I think I do – I've read several books on the subject and that seems to me by far the best reason for these sorts of images to come up."

Confronted with self-analysis like this on the part of the narrator, I always feel, as a reader, as if the writer has just turned away from the page. It's the difference between opening up a world in such a way that it becomes available to all of us ("interestingly personal", you could say) and dropping that endeavour (in a way that none of the writers I've quoted here does) in order to pursue some insight into him or herself, instead. Should you ever wonder if that's happening in your own writing, simply test whatever you're writing for the presence of specific, sensuous detail. Those details make what's being written available to all of us. They're what lifts the material beyond reach of what you might claim as being about you, and therefore out of the context of what's of interest to you alone.

An unsigned article from *The New Yorker* expresses this distinction memorably, and I find that I turn to it on those days when I wonder if fiction-writing, memoir, or any other kind of writing really helps anyone at all:

Details are the stuff of fiction. They either attract or repel [...] Details are also the stuff of a humanistic perspective. Ambiguous and unpredictable, details undermine ideology. They are connective. They hook your interest in a way that ideas never can. If you let in the details of some aspect of life, you almost have to allow that aspect to be what it really is rather than what you want or need it to be. And yet details are also mysteriously universal. If fiction is news, it is largely news about the details of other lives, but if fiction has a vital interest for people, it's because in those details, they somehow get news of themselves. The readiness to be interested in the details of lives unlike one's own is a profound measure of trust. Resisting details is usually an expression of xenophobia, of some insecurity and shyness, of a need to keep safely to oneself.[23]

Does the writing connect, or shut out? Is it boringly self-centred, or interestingly personal? Look to the sensuous detail.

Writing Experience

FREEFALL WRITING

For now, don't worry about giving too much sensuous detail. Tip far over onto that side of the bicycle if you need to. Write without a conscious plan, as the first precept advises, and if you get the idea as you write that you know where you're going, don't rush there: stay with it moment by moment, and find out by writing whether that's where you actually end up.

Continue to write for at least an hour every day, going where the energy is for you, and not changing anything. Select some of the work to share with your writing partner, if you have one.

Writing Tip: Specific detail is far more effective than habitual detail. Instead of "we used to", or "we would always", name a specific day and make it the one time this particular event will ever happen. ("That Tuesday, we …")

TIMED WRITING

These are exercises you can do alone, with a timer, or with your writing partner. But let yourself write them at different times, in different situations, for varying lengths of time: at midnight, at 4 a.m., in a park or in a crowded restaurant. As vital as it is to have a routine, it's also good to let your psyche know that you don't depend on it.

1.
a) Christmas traditions at our house were …
b) What made this Christmas different from all the rest was …

2.
a) My parents had their own way of "keeping up with the Joneses"
b) One day at our house the neighbours will never forget was …
(You can see what I'm getting at. Now make up some of your own.)

3.
a) Write about an event involving someone you only dimly remember
b) Now write an event in which you and that person are much more
   actively involved

4. Star gazing
5. Earthquake!
6. Never again

Writing Tip: If you don't remember a specific detail, make it up.
Remember, beyond certain key features, you're making it up anyway.
And there are no memory police. Let your motto be, "Just say ..."

Chapter Five
Dropping In, with Sensuous Detail

What do we know except what we've seen, felt, drunk, heard and touched. What else do we know?

- Farley Mowat

Having taken a closer look at the implications of the third precept, "Give all the sensuous detail", in relation to the first, "Write what comes up for you", I would like to take some time to talk about the third precept in its own right, and its essential role in opening up the world that the writing – and the writer – inhabits.

Moving from Telling to Showing

When you're writing and you find yourself summarising an event or a story that comes up rather than going directly into what you (or your characters) can see, feel, hear, taste, smell and touch there – stop. Take a deep breath, and begin to open up those sensuous details, proceeding from moment to moment in the scene in front of you. Even if you're trying to give the sense of the whole arc of a relationship, as people often do, don't get mired in background and build-up. Go straight to the scenes (the experiences) that have the most energy for you and give the sensuous details of those scenes. That way, you'll be showing the relationship in action, rather than talking *about* it, and you'll be right inside. To use a faithful old writing distinction that was first drawn almost 100 years ago,[24] it's the difference between "telling" (summarising) and "showing": going into the specific details that will put you (and, incidentally, your reader) right there.

I think you may be quite surprised at some of what comes up when you really start to do this: new things that were not at all in your mind when you started. The fact is that when you stand back and "tell", you're also to a great extent exerting control – or trying to exert control – over the action. But when you "show", the world you're writing about starts to take over, and you begin to feel almost as if you're its servant, faithfully recording what goes on there, instead. And that's when it really becomes exciting.

I sometimes wonder if I should even describe how this works, because it happens quite spontaneously in many people's writing. They're writing along, moving pretty quickly over the territory ("telling"), when all of a sudden they seem almost to get lost in some specific, sensuous detail. It's at that very moment that the writing drops in, and the next thing I see is that they're moving slowly and moment by moment through an event and a landscape that's richly "shown" – usually in some way that it's clear to me they haven't anticipated. The world they're writing about has taken over.

It's not easy for me to give you an example of this happening, because it's a process that usually takes place over several pages. But I will try to do that here by giving you some excerpts from the "telling" in this piece by Terry Van Luyk. The section begins (as I'm sure many people would like to) with the statement, "I'm in a panic now. I can't submit nothing." Quickly, she scrabbles around in the area of family, generalising:

When you are one of five kids who've all been born within six years of one another a lot of shit happens. Shit at school like getting compared to one another and labelled with an attribute that sticks for life. Shit at home because your mother had too many kids and, by her own admission,

54

wished she'd just stayed on the farm she worked at when she first arrived in Canada and raised animals instead. Shit amongst the relatives who have to differentiate you from your multitude of siblings and so give you a nickname like "Chubby", which in my brother's hands transformed into "fat pig" and became the only moniker I was addressed by at home.

Realising, I think, that she's trapped herself in a very broad summary, this writer focuses in on the I-character, but she's still generalising. The following is a list of things the I-character "would" do (in general), rather than something specific she "did" do on a particular day. (Please understand that I'm not saying that it's wrong to write this way. Writing this passage is exactly what got this writer where she needed to go. I'm talking about the contrast between this kind of "telling" and the "showing" that will come.)

I was the worrier, the nervous one who cracked her knuckles, blinked a thousand times a minute and had to do things in threes: things like opening the back door or pulling down the sheets to get into bed at night. All of my nervous ticks were obvious to anyone nearby and so I had to devise ways to cover them up. I'd pretend to change my mind a few times before going out and that way I could put on my shoes three times and get into my coat three times. Is it any wonder they put me into the slow class at school. Twice.

Quickly, she takes the narrative to a more specific situation: a game the teacher of the slow class would (still general) have the children play about how many coins it took to make change – a game the I-character excelled at.

If she went over a dollar and said "one dollar and sixteen cents" a lot of the kids would forget about the fifty cent pieces and I could shoot my hand up before anyone else. Once in a while she would buy chocolate bars as prizes and one time I won the Aero bar.

Now at last, with that "one time", she's able to close in on a specific situation. And look what happens when she allows herself to dwell on the sensuous details of eating the Aero bar:

It was just before recess and I took it out with me because I couldn't wait for lunch. Besides if I took it home at lunch my brother would steal it from me and eat all of it. Slowly I put my arms into my coat sleeves, slowly I tugged my winter boots on, taking my time so that my friends wouldn't wait for me any longer and I could be alone. I stood in the foyer between the sets of double doors, which was out of bounds during recess, so that the wind wouldn't whip around me and disturb the full effect of eating an entire chocolate bar. I took my first bite, not allowing myself to bite beyond the line that demarcated the next square. It was sugary and light unlike my favourite chocolate bar, the Snickers. I worried that once I got to the end I wouldn't feel all of it in my stomach, that there were too many air holes in the bar. Next time, I'd have to win earlier than anyone else so that I could choose the Sweet Marie bar. Mrs. Jones didn't buy Snickers. Maybe I could let her know that probably lots of kids would pick that as their favourite. Mom would slap me for saying that, telling me that would be rude and that the only proper response is a heartfelt thank you.

Shelley Ray opens the door from outside.

Suddenly, Shelley Ray appears – a character I feel very sure was not in this writer's mind when she started.

She's wearing a ratty old coat that probably six or seven of her sisters wore before her. Her family has even more kids than mine, but they didn't come from the Catholic school.

"Going to the washroom, Shelley?" I ask hopefully.

"Just getting out of the wind," she replies. I've hidden the bar behind me. Mom's rule is that you never eat in front of anyone unless you offer them some of what you have. I don't want to share my Aero bar. Shelley might expect half of it. The bar is getting soft under my fingertips and I shuffle them down a little so I don't melt it.

"Is it good?" she asks and I nod my head. We stare at each other.

"Who are you playing with?" I ask.

"No one," she replies.

Shelley Ray has large eyes. They don't leave me. She is still and quiet, as though she is accustomed to waiting for things. I feel so mad at her for invading my privacy, ruining my chocolate moment, making me feel guilty *and greedy. Go away, Shelley Ray, I want to say to her but I couldn't bear to see the hurt on her face.*

I shift away from the heater's grill that starts to blast hot air into the foyer. The bell won't ring for another ten minutes and I don't know what to do.

"You can eat it," she says to me and I feel something in my stomach that is heavy, but not from the one square of chocolate. I nibble up to the next line and then put the bar behind my back again. I really should give her one square. Just one. That wouldn't be so hard at all. I take another bite.

"Is it good?" she asks again.

I nod.

I won't give the final twist away, in case this scene makes it into a story someday – and in any case the point is clear. Concentrating on the specific, sensuous details of starting to eat the Aero bar, all the way down to the first demarcation line, brings the writer into the writing in a whole new way. And with that, there appears to the I-character the unexpected figure of someone from an even bigger family, with even fewer expectations, even more deprived – her large-eyed, quiet shadow, Shelley Ray. After the pell-mell rush of the first few paragraphs, it feels like such a luxury to be able to sink into one scene in this way, and to be with this very specific, detailed action as it takes its own direction from one moment to the next.

Showing Through "Opening Out"

Often, when people have already done quite a lot of this kind of writing, I give an exercise called "opening out", in which I ask them to go back to a piece they've already written and "show" what they've "told" (summarised or interpreted), at a place I specify.

The results, once that narrative control has been removed, can be quite astonishing. Sometimes (perhaps for fear of stepping directly into the emotions felt by some past self), people have chosen the general over the specific – to stay with the habitual past ("we would go"), for example (a point I broached in the first writing tip at the end of the last chapter), rather than write about a specific day. But the effect of talking about repeated actions in the past – the way things usually tended to go – is one of standing a long way back from those actions, remaining firmly in the point of view of the narrator in the present. Have a look, for example, at this excerpt from Peggie Merlin's writing:

After study hall, we would climb the hill to the girls' dorm. Because it had been the manor house of a fine estate in a former time, there was a kitchen. We would pack into it and there, like swarming bees, settle upon the pails of cold morning toast and the industrial-size barrels of peanut butter. It is a mystery how this might have represented the comforts of home, since my home was a desert for "pop" food. Maybe it was the very contrast - a Jiffy rebellion? - that made it so satisfying. I would slather and down three, sometimes four shingles of toast before turning in. I was 98 lbs. on Labor Day and 130 by Christmas. I went from a training bra to a 36B in three months!

Although the glimpse of what went on in the kitchen is vivid (helped along by the image of their settling "like swarming bees" on the toast and peanut butter), the scene is cast as part of the habitual past and therefore remains general. And the point of view is very much that of the adult narrator who now looks back, explains, generalises about and queries the action (some of this is "a mystery" to her, but she can also think – now – of a possible explanation). In other words, it's primarily "telling".

In order to shift the style of narrative to "showing", I wrote in the margin, "Take me into one of those nights in the kitchen." This is what she wrote in response:

The snow had been falling thickly for some time when the bell released us. I pulled on my boots without taking off my tennis shoes, grabbed my parka, pulled up the hood, wrapped my arms around the stack of books and notes and headed up the hill toward the dorm whose lights beckoned more than a 1/4 mile away. The warmth of the lovely house was only part of the reward. Inside a merry jostle of pink cheeked girls packed the only room not filled with beds and jockeyed for position. It was a generous kitchen - although the stove no longer functioned. At its center, like an altar, a table lay set with the evening offering: pails of peanut butter and dry toast.

"Move over," I said, reaching deep into the plastic toast bucket and hooking a couple of pieces for the sake of efficiency. To reach the second station, where the peanut butter waited, I had to push through at least a dozen girls. I knew I would need a glass of water at some point in this sacrament, but that would come later. I did not want to wait another minute. I was ravenous. I didn't care if my mouth got stuck half shut, did not care if I could not speak. Or breathe. Or swallow. Or even hear. Oh, God, how could I be this hungry? And night after night?

When you focus on a specific moment in time, it becomes much more difficult to "tell". In this version, the adult narrator, looking back, has all but vanished, and instead we're firmly in the point of view of the girl herself, taking part in the action. You'll notice that this passage is much richer in sensuous detail from the outset, has dialogue (a specific, sensuous detail to be sure), and moves from one moment to the next. We've lost the lovely image of swarming bees, but it's been replaced by another (for me, far more emotionally charged) one – that of the toast and peanut butter as a sacrament. By the end, with the I-character willing almost to suffocate as she chokes down the food, no-one needs to query why she would eat like this. Her question seems rhetorical. We've been through the experience ourselves as we read about it, and emotionally, we already know.

Obviously, it's not an exact science. "Showing" and "telling" are a matter of degree. But even if you're already in the habit of opening quite far into the sensuous detail in your writing, you may discover that it's possible for you to become more immersed in whatever world you find yourself writing about by becoming even more specific.

Still on the theme of adolescent girls together, here is an example of a scene (by Julie Gittus) that's already sensuously detailed and specific, but yields up even more of its complexity by becoming more so.

The game started on a rainy day.

Gayle lay on her bed, picking at the chenille bedspread cover while I lay on mine reading comic romances. She dug out the pen and paper from the scrabble box under the bed and began to make lists. There was my list and her list. Two columns – my name topping one, hers the other. We each swore to tell the truth. At the beginning it was simple and childish. Favourite animal. *Favourite colour. Worst name. Best name. Most loved thing. Most scary thing.* I let the words burst out before I had a chance to censure them:

Growing pubes.

Gayle tittered as she wrote. I realised then it was a list we would have to shred as soon as it was completed. She didn't look at me as she whispered:

"Well I'm looking forward to it. When I grow mine I am going to wash them with shampoo and comb and brush them."

We both erupted into giggles, uncontrollable giggling. I thought I would piss myself we giggled so much, each of us rolling around on the beds and stuffing pillows over our faces to muffle the noise. Her answer shocked and comforted me all at once. The fact she had even thought about it – gone to the point of making plans even. She must be as wicked as I was.

Because I couldn't really sense much difference between the two girls in the piece, and I wanted to know more – at least about the I-character – before the main event happened, I put an "open-out mark" (>) beside "reading comic romances". This is what she wrote:

I'd bought them down at the newsagency the day before. Already I had read them so often I almost knew all the dialogue by heart. The men were always tall with muscly chests and arms – a bit like the man in the Chesty Bonds advertisement - while the women were slim with pointy upright breasts. I studied the pictures closely. Even when the characters lifted their arms there was never any evidence of hair. All chests and legs were hairless as well. This observation worried me.

I folded my knees into triangles and propped the comic on top of my bony mountains. Gayle had started scraping at her nails with a metal nail file. I hated the noise. It made me feel a twitchy sort of tightness in my cheeks and mouth. And I hated the fact that although Gayle was only ten - a whole year younger than me – she actually had nails to file. Mine were nibbled back to the quick. I stopped staring at my comic and looked across at her. She was now sitting cross-legged on her camp bed and I could just make out her nails. They were the same mauve pink colour that I sometimes found on the inside of shells. Little white half-moons decorated their bases. They were beautiful nails. I clenched my fists to hide mine away.

"Can you quit it?" I asked her.

Gayle held her cupped fingers towards herself and huffed air. I could smell the faint sulphury smell now of ground fingernails. Then she dropped the file on the chenille bedspread and looked across at me.

"Finished anyway," she said. "And besides, I've got a great idea for a game."

Along with the increased specificity of sensuous detail (the sound of the nails being filed, the "twitchy sort of tightness" in the I-character's cheeks) comes a much greater degree of closeness to the action, as well as much more clarity about the difference between the two girls. Whether or not the added information about the comic books adds anything to the piece in itself, I have the sense that the mere fact of spending more time with them allows the writer to re-enter the action of the piece much more slowly, and that in turn allows for the emergence of the nail-filing, and all that it implies to the I-character, along the way. In fact, if you look at it closely, the comic book paragraph itself remains somewhat general, in the "they would always" mode. It would be interesting to see what another "open out" mark beside "I almost knew all the dialogue by heart" would bring. But perhaps I'm getting carried away.

My purpose in showing you these "opened out" passages is not to suggest that you go back and "open out" the passages of "telling" in your own writing right now. In fact, I would suggest that you *not* do that: I think it's far too early in the process for that kind of looking back to be done cleanly, without re-awakening some of the dragons of criticism that you've just begun to put to sleep. My purpose is to show you the difference in effect between showing and telling on you, as a writer, and to invite you to begin to slow down and open out *as you* write. In the writing directives that follow, I've given some reminders that you can carry over into your daily practice. In the timed exercises, you'll find topics that could well provoke some "telling", but this time, you're being asked to "show". Each time you find yourself pulling back into generalisations, or slipping into the "would" of the habitual past, turn instead to the specifics: "that day" instead of "those days", "we did" instead of "we would do". Focus on one scene, one incident instead of an overview, and watch to see if you're entering into the sensuous detail.

If you're not already in the habit of doing these things, you may feel terribly exposed at first. What you're doing is letting go of the illusion of control over the story, and over how the material will be interpreted. But it's helpful to remember that that sense of control is, at best, an illusion. Actually, the more you tell someone how to think about something, the more they'll begin to wonder about the opposite. In letting go of that attempt, you're acquiescing to the fact that, as Jacques Lacan pointed out, language is "a presence made of absence"[25] – although you can know what you're saying, *you can never know how it will be heard*. Now is the time, as you experiment with "showing", to begin to let go of even the illusion that you can tell another person how to respond to what you write.

Writing Experience

FREEFALL WRITING

Continue writing for an hour every day, and see what comes up. Go toward whatever has energy for you, and don't fall into the trap of giving lots of background. When you find yourself summarising, generalising, or talking "about" some experience, stop. Go directly to the specific, moment-by-moment sensuous detail of one scene from the experience and immerse yourself in that. And don't forget dialogue (direct speech: "He said, 'x'" rather than indirect speech: "He said that he…"). Dialogue is a specific, sensuous detail.

If writing close up in this way ("showing") feels different to you from writing about an experience through an overlay of the thoughts you have about that experience now, you may find it helpful to make some notes about how it feels different, and share them with your writing partner. Whether or not you have a writing partner, enter that information in your writing journal, where you record your writing experiences and discoveries as they arise.

NB: If you think you would like to continue some scene or story you began the day before, begin to write and see if that's what comes up for you. If not, leave it for now. If it's really important to you, it'll come up again one of these days.

Writing Tip: If you often decide that you "don't have time" to go into some of the things that come up in your writing, set aside two two-hour writing periods each week this month, when you *will* have time to enter fully into whatever comes up. "Not having time" is one of the major engines of avoidance for all of us these days. But the reality is, you can find the time.

TIMED WRITING

As always, you can do these exercises alone or with your writing partner, but time them. 15-20 minutes should be enough for each one. Keep in mind the need to go directly to a specific situation, moment by moment, in all its sensuous detail, even when the subject has to do with repetition.

1. Caught in a lie
2. Breaking the law
3. Unforgivable
4. Making the best of a bad situation
5. "To want, to want, to want, and not to have"(from Virginia Woolf, *The Waves*)
6. Choose me!

Writing Tip: Bear in mind this advice: "Never retract, never explain, never apologise. Just get the job done and let them howl!"[26]

Chapter Six
Finding Where the Energy Is

How do you discover, on any given day, where the energy is for you in the writing? It's very much like dowsing. You're walking (or writing) along, hands on the willow branch (or the keyboard), and just noticing, just feeling it out. All of a sudden, you feel the branch shiver and dip. There's energy down there. You stop and sense further. Now you're holding onto the branch for all you're worth, and it's still jerking and dipping down, down toward the ground. Do you drop the branch, run in the other direction, and dig your well as fast as you can in the opposite corner of the field? Not if you want to find water, you don't. You dig where your hands and the willow branch are telling you to dig. You dig where the water is.

Your body will know when something has energy for you – there's a tug or a thrill, a jolt, a tension that's visceral. Or maybe it's just a vague sense of unease. But from that point on, it's up to you. Do you stay there and dig, or run away?

For many of us, the first response to that lurch of excitement is something like dread: "I can't write about that." The mind throws up a myriad reasons: it's too old, it hasn't composted enough, it's too personal, it's too weird, it's too ordinary, nobody will understand it, everyone will hate me. But what those reasons all basically elaborate is the same powerful uncertainty: "I'm afraid of what will happen if I go there."

What I'm saying by means of the fourth precept, "Go where the energy is, or go fearward," is that that very energy, that charge of anxiety, is your signal that this is precisely the place *to* go. The fact that the writing that emerges when you do so is virtually guaranteed to be absorbing to a reader is almost beside the point. What's vitally important, in my view, is the fact that the writing you do when you delve into that place will grip *you*, and that absorption will teach you more about writing, more quickly, than any other means I could suggest.

Finding Out What You Don't Know

To me, the very fact that such an energy can be sensed at all indicates the presence of an edge to what is known and comfortable – and of an area beyond that edge that is in some sense available (and dare I say ripe) for discovery. This unknown may have to do with content (in that you don't know what you will find there), or it may have to do with technique (in that you don't know whether you're capable of what might be demanded of you technically, once you get there). But the choice to proceed in that direction anyway is exactly the sort of choice I was referring to in the introduction, when I said that surrender in writing means "learning how to allow your willing, intending self to get out of the way, so that a deeper level of vulnerability becomes possible". "The whole language of writing" as James Baldwin points out, "[...] is finding out what you don't want to know, what you don't want to find out. But something forces you to anyway."[27] Here is your chance to let the writing take you beyond what you know.

There is no use imagining what might await you there. *Writing will take you to different places from those you can reach by thinking.* But your sense that a particular subject or area has energy for you on a given day is a trustworthy companion in the process. You know where you need to go, even if it seems impossible. You know what you need to do, even if it takes a considerable amount of courage to follow through.

I would like to give you a couple of examples of how powerful the writing can be if you do turn toward the energy that is there for you, *even though that may seem impossible* to you when you begin. Often the individual triumphs that I see taking place can't be quoted to good effect in a context like this because they're lengthy or cumulative, but these two short pieces will give you an impressive indication of the level of attainment I mean.

What follows is a piece written by someone for whom finding what had energy seemed to mean entering a reality that she couldn't grasp and hold still long enough to write about. Before she even attempted the passage I'm about to quote below, she wrote:

It's not that I can't think of something to write about, it's that I think of too many things to write about at once and can't slow my brain down enough to crystallize a single [thing] alone, by itself. That's not exactly true, either. I can sometimes quickly squeeze out a moment, a fragment of time, a remembered pain. But only so briefly, so condensed and thick, like thawed frozen orange juice straight from the can. As if adding the water would take too long, or let the words too easily slip through me. And the moment would be gone. Where do those moments go.
(Beverley Stapleton)

That said, she went on to write:

... Back, back, back always back. Back behind doors and under beds; hidden at the back of small dark narrow front hall cupboards. Squished up into tiny balls of tucked in arms and legs and little heads that can't be reached. Trying not to breathe. Praying in the most silent holy prayers that God will come and take me home. I am a child of God. He will not abandon me. Now and at the hour of our death ...
"Get your hand off my ass." I feel the words through the wall, red mad, don't touch me words. They are fighting again.
I pull the blankets closer but I know I will not stay in my bed.
"Ahh, Jesus Chris Janet, let's have some." He slurs loudly, half laughing.
"Get off. Get the hell off me." She shouts back. I can hear her moving off the bed.
"Oh, I see then, what's this about then, eh? Bloody hell! I don't think so!"

His voice getting louder, madder as I hear his body bump up against the wall and his feet heavy steps now on the floor. Her scream slices right through the wall.

I'm out of my bed and at their door before I know I have done this, before her tears come.

I push the door open slowly and tell him not to hurt mummy. I stand there waiting, looking at him then at mummy crying against the dressing table. He shouts at me and I jump. "Get back to bed, and mind your own business, miss smarty-pants." I freeze. I say once more, "Don't hurt mummy."

"I'll show you what I can and cannot do." As he reaches for his pants crumpled up on the chair in the corner, grabbing for his thick, black belt.

I turn and run but I don't know where I am running.

Mummy cries, "Oh Jesus, Richard don't, not now, it's the middle of the night, leave her be."

"Get out of my way or I'll give you a taste of this too," he shouts back at her as I hear his huge heavy steps coming fast behind me.

My bedroom is still very dark but my eyes know the dark. I move very fast to squeeze in behind a place where he cannot find me. I make myself very, very small; a little ball of tucked in arms and legs and head pulled down tight to my chest. My heart so loud I start to pray that it is beating straight to God and I am not in this body anymore. I am trying not to breathe, not move, not to be at all.

A cold, flat snap loud and close jerks my head up and I start to shake. My tummy tight and hurting from being squished starts pushing pains down inside. I am trying not to cry.

I feel his hand on the collar of my pajama top as I try to pull away, but he catches a handful of my hair. I resist the pulling until I feel some of the hair give way in his big fingers.

But he comes back quickly now both hands, my whole head, I cannot pull; he is pulling me up, out from behind my dresser. One hand now is dragging me across the floor, onto the bed.

"Think you're so clever, do you?" I can tell he is talking with his teeth closed together even though my face is against the mattress. "Well, this'll teach you to be so clever, this'll remind you to stay out of it. It's none of your godamn business, you hear me?" As he rips my pajama pants down and presses my back into the bed.

Whack, whack, whack, whack, whack, whack.

"You hear me?"

The result of exploring one of those brief, "condensed and thick" moments, I think you'll agree, is a scene of formidably sustained tension and spare, evocative dialogue. Above all, it keeps the reader immersed in the character's perspective, virtually throughout. Despite lamenting that the moment couldn't be captured, couldn't be "thawed", this writer has turned toward the flash of energy she felt there. And far from disappearing under scrutiny, that moment has opened up a whole world, and taken us irrevocably inside.

The following (in some ways oddly similar) piece, first written as an in-class exercise, seemed impossible to the writer to accomplish technically. In fact, she was in tears after she had written it because of what she perceived to be her inability to do it justice. When I later found that piece of writing, not much changed, serving as the climax to her first published novel, I felt very happy to see it there; given time, she had clearly come to recognise what she had achieved. Although it's impossible to capture the impact it has in the novel by quoting it out of context, I think the writing is also very powerful on its own:

I swallow. I watch. I breathe fast. I hear Doreen closing the nursery door. I can't hear them any more, I can't hear their voices. I lie waiting in the cold silence trying not to imagine, trying not to feel or see or breathe, trying not to exist, but the horrifying feeling of something slipping in beside me makes me whisper a low squeal.

"Angel of God!" I whisper. "Angel of God, my guardian dear." I can't remember it, I can't remember the prayer. "Angel of God, my guardian dear ..." The feelings are in my throat, I daren't breathe them in, bristling slippery monsters, eyes that look at you. "Angel of God, my guardian dear, ever this night be at my side ... ever this night be at my side." I am whispering it out loud, my feet are feeling each other in panicking circles, I want to cry out, to scream, but then they would have me, they would lift me out of my bed. "Angel of God, BE AT MY SIDE." I can feel tears on my cheek, my body quivers, the terror is sharp and cold. "Angel of God." I begin to sob quietly. "Angel of God," I beg.

Suddenly with a clap, it is there, standing in the thundering silence of its outstretched wings. It is lit by gold threads. It flickers. Diamond shapes of black and gold and green are on its dress.

I know it is there for me.

I draw my knees up to my chin and squeeze my eyes shut.

But I do not sleep, and into the trembling of my half-awake dream a voice speaks:

"I am the red earth and
the green shoot,
the orange-bellied newt in
the swollen water.
I am the howling night
and the first light,
the blue dusk, and the
twisted root.
I am the lashing rain,
the spotted egg,
the hissing flame.
Look for me in sunlit water shadows and the grass in dew,
seek me in the hearts of flowers and the gentle sound of doves,
for I am with you.
I am with you along black corridors and by the edge of the black chasm.
I am with you in the lonely darkness and the longing of the day
and I hold you with the stillness of the hills."

(Helena McEwen, *The Big House*)

Going Fearward

I give "Go where the energy is" primacy over "Go fearward" in this precept, precisely because I don't want you to limit your sensing – your dowsing – *only* to the experience of fear, which I can't believe any writer sustains every day. There are going to be days, of course, when you do want to write about what comes up for you. And there are bound to be days on which every direction that presents itself to you, as you write, feels flat or smooth or easy, or even dull. Does that mean that you're so relaxed in the writing process that nothing has an edge for you any more?

I don't think so. My guess is that the act of turning away from an emergent energy may be happening so fast that you're simply not aware of it. So if you find yourself in one of these "no energy" situations, my suggestion – as a kind of shortcut – is: "Go fearward". Write something you know you're reluctant or afraid to write about. You will find there's plenty of energy tied up there.

When you do "go fearward", three things, typically, will tend to happen. First, you may get an excellent opportunity to see one of the many faces of your internal critic, one of the "dragons at the gate". Take a moment and jot down what that internal critic is telling you. Although that critic will probably never go away entirely, the content of its messages will change over time, and it's a good idea to become acquainted with them.

The second thing that will happen, once you step past that critic, is that something will get written. My bet is that it will be powerful writing. I'm not saying that you'll be happy with it at the time. On the contrary, as was the case even for the author of the remarkable piece you've just read, writing what we fear to write often seems to result in writing that looks terrible to us – completely unacceptable – until we're able to hear and believe someone else's response to it. But once it can be considered from the perspective that comes with time, this writing virtually always turns out to be work that the author is proud of, or considers to have been very worthwhile.[28]

The third thing that typically results from "going fearward" is that the degree of focus you will have had to muster in order to get something written at all will have taught you something very valuable about self-forgetfulness in writing. Think back to the piece you've just read about the child who is beaten. What began with "I don't" and "I can't" and "I can sometimes quickly squeeze out a moment", became a sustained and gripping scene in which the trepidations of the adult narrator were nowhere to be found. Recall how quickly "I lost a couple of friends by drowning, but I don't have much to say about it" turned into a richly evocative account of that journey, in the piece I quoted in Chapter Four. What has happened above all for these writers, I believe, is that they've forgotten themselves in the writing by dint of sheer absorption in what they're writing about. Writing against the edge of their fear and refusal has required that they focus in closely on the subject in order to write at all. And then, once they're inside that world, they keep going in order to keep on finding out what happens there.

Over time, the repeated experience of this degree of absorption will lead to a solid trust in the writing process – to the development of a part of you that knows that you will write, that it is safe to be taken over by it, and that however you feel in the process, you will keep on writing. It's the experience of this trusting witness, as I think of it, that will override the internal critic, time after time, and allow you to write that which arises to be written. This is something that will happen spontaneously, as you continue to write. But my fear is that without repeated experience of "going where the energy is for you" it will take a very long time – perhaps too long – for that vitally important faith in writing to emerge.

Balancing

Soon after I introduce the third precept, "Give all the sensuous detail", someone will often protest – even as he is discovering what worlds the use of sensuous detail can unlock for him – "I don't like to read a lot of sensuous detail. It bores me. What I like is to have a lot happening in what I read." But as I mentioned when I first outlined these guidelines, it's important to remember that although it's useful to introduce them separately, in the writing they work *together*. To go back to the bicycle analogy, if too much sensuous detail has you tipping the bicycle over to one side, writing what has energy for you will certainly help you to right it. When you're writing right up against the kind of edge we've been talking about here, the extent to which you become absorbed in the writing, and compelled to move forward by the events that are taking place, means that an excess of detail is almost impossible to achieve.

Have a look at what happens in this piece of writing with regard to sensuous detail. This writer was facing down the dragon of "everyone will hate me", I suspect, once it became clear to him where he was going to have to go. Time has moved on since this subject was embraced with any enthusiasm, even though the point he is making is a contemporary one – and as I recall, a young woman ran from the room as I finished reading it out. I think many of us would have preferred not to have heard it. Yet for this writer, writing what turned out to have energy on this day taught him a great deal about what it means to balance those precepts. And the strength of our reactions was a testament as much to the way the piece is written, as to the (to me) agonising content of what he found he had to write.

The writer begins with the I-character, a 15-year-old boy, cleaning his guns in preparation for a trip to his father's property in the country – guns that he details lovingly, from the .22, to the Armalite (a semi-automatic military rifle) to his own .22, "exactly what a boy needed to feel complete as he roamed the bush. [...] You didn't need anything else, you didn't need, or want, anyone with you when you wandered, just your .22 and the ammo belt, tracking down roos, wallabies, rabbits, the odd exotic bird." There is a quite a lot of sensuous detail concerning the feel and the look of these guns, but it's necessary, I think, to draw the writer himself into the world of the piece.

It is the Armalite that is at first at the centre of the story. "They said when it hit a man the hole in the front of his chest was normal, but his back was blown out where the bullet came through. Mum had her doubts about me taking this one with me", but "Dad assured her of my good sense". Soon we're at the landing of the old woolshed where he tries to impress a couple of young locals from the next property with his "city firepower". What follows is a relatively comic scene in which he discharges thirty rounds of expensive ammunition from the Armalite toward a "mob of roos" and fails to hit any of them, blasting "the hills into disbelief", after which "the neighbour's kids wandered off home", unimpressed.

The writer might have preferred to end it there. But some impulse was drawing him on, so he followed it.

I was following the creek up into the hills. The scrub was closing in and darkening towards dusk. The best time for roos. The .22 hung comfortably across my back, the strap across my chest. I liked it close so it didn't flap or slip around as I climbed over the granite boulders and further into the hills. I moved quietly, placing my feet on soft ground to muffle my footfall, stepping over twigs and leaves in silence. There was a calm expectancy in that walk. I was sure I'd come across something before dark.

It was the movement of its head, lifting to watch me that caught my eye. Its head up, it stared motionless at me, leaving its drinking from the little pool as it spotted me. I froze at the same time, taking in my luck and its beauty. It was a swamp wallaby, glossy black coat, crouching slightly from its drinking. It watched me intently, its eyes dark brown in its elegant head. Smaller all over than a grey roo, with a more rounded head, softer lines in its snout. Ears also more rounded, showing a little reddy brown through the membrane. It watched me intently, without fear. I liked the way it looked at me, made me feel part of the bush, not an intruder, but another creature of the bush.

Lowering the rifle had to be smooth, not allowing the gun to be seen as separate from me. Even as I ducked slightly to lift the strap over my head it just watched. I was holding it with my eyes, not fifty yards away. I raised the rifle, smoothly, face expressionless, cocked it, lined the wallaby up in the sights. A perfect shot. It watched me still, stared back at me, back through the sights, right back into my eyes, into me. For seconds we stayed like that, eye to eye, wallaby to boy, creature to creature, both motionless. Both captured in silence. I lowered the barrel slightly, to take in its heart. Its head was too small. The wallaby stayed with me as I eased the trigger in. I dreaded what I was about to do, and didnt stop. The finger pulled. The trigger passed the first pressure. It flowed slow motion into the ghastly explosion that came with it.

Why hadnt it died? It was an easy shot. Blood ran from its wound in the upper chest, bright red over glossy black. It lay on its side as I looked down on it. It was still watching me, panting gently. I cursed it for not dying. Dropped the gun, picked up a thick stick. It didnt take its eyes off me as I brought the club down on its head. Again and again. It wouldnt die. It wouldnt close its eyes. How could this be? Death came on us excruciatingly slowly, drawn out, easing into death, despite the blows from the stick. It eased into death, separate from its pain, as I stood over it, crying out at its wilfulness, at my cruelty, never condemning me, accepting those blows as it went in its own time, that gentle, steady solitary teacher.

(Peter Becke)

With a scene this emotionally searing, it's not easy to pay attention to the way the scene is written. But if you look back, you'll quickly see that once the boy catches sight of the creature, the forward impulse of the piece slows down almost to a standstill. At that point, there is a wealth of sensuous detail about the wallaby – its coat, the shape of its head, the colour of the light through its ears – the very timing of which prepares us for the frozen stillness that will accompany the act of killing itself. The fact that from the moment the predator spots his prey, the tension of our not wanting (and ultimately his not wanting) this act to occur, never lets up, means that the moment-by-moment rendering of sensuous detail surrounding the act is effortless to sustain.

Even if you find you need to give what feels like too much sensuous detail, in order to bring yourself far enough into the world you're writing about to know what has energy for you there, then I say go ahead and do it. That's an important part of the process. Be assured that if you're really able to go to the places that do have energy, or to "go fearward", you're unlikely to have to worry about an excess of detail. You're far more likely to be gripped by what you're writing, with results that are clear and incisive – absorbing, without a word to spare.

Lost in the Funhouse?

I prayed to rediscover my childhood, and it has come back, and I feel that it is just as difficult as it used to be, and that growing older has served no purpose at all.
- Rainer Maria Rilke, *The Notebooks of Malte Laurids Brigge*

When people have just begun to write, and everything that comes by seems to serve as a distraction, I sometimes see them make comments in their writing to the effect of, "If *only* I could become so absorbed in what I'm writing that I got lost in it." But within a relatively short time, as they continue, I find them writing about drowning, being overtaken by rapids, falling off a mountain, failing to read a map properly, getting lost in the woods, or other similar disasters. When that happens, I can't help inferring that at some level these writers are experiencing a fear of losing themselves in the writing, or – to put it another way – of entering into the perspective of another character (a past self, for instance) and getting stuck there, like the father in Ray Bradbury's chilling short story, *The Playground*, who trades his adulthood to become a child again in that terrifying, Darwinian jungle of the bullies and the bullied, to spare his own child the torture of having to do so.

What I've discovered over the years is that although the ego has many ways of throwing that particular fear into the path of writing (especially when the writing is autobiographical), it's not actually something that can happen. Painful feelings do sometimes come up, but as long as the writer doesn't let them bring the writing to a halt, they can be experienced and moved through in a way that feels worthwhile. But as for getting lost or stuck in some sort of altered or regressed state, experience has shown me that with writing, that simply doesn't happen.

One way I have found to understand this is by referring to the model for Transactional Analysis, which centres on transactions within the psyche among three ego states: the "parent" – a construct comprised of what as children we think constitutes being wise and grown up, whether affirming or critical; the "child" – the playful, ungoverned, wilful, creative part; and the "adult" – that aspect which performs the more mature, compassionate, synthesising functions. What seems to me to happen in writing is that even if the writer does enter into the perspective of the "child", *the act of writing itself functions as the "adult"* – shaping, synthesising and witnessing what goes on for that ego-state (or character), just as a therapist provides the "adult" presence for whatever regression or personality shift the client undertakes.

I am not saying that writing in this way *is* therapy, because although it may have therapeutic side effects, the focus here is on writing rather than on healing the writer. What I am saying is that the ever-present fact that writing is taking place means that the adult is present, synthesising, ordering, seeing further. And as long as that is the case, writers can't get trapped or lost in any of their other ego-states, no matter how real that possibility may appear to them at the time.

And yet, with regard to the fourth precept, I can't help wondering, what is it that creates this energy that indicates a direction for the writing? What is it that draws us on? My hunch is that it's an innate urge to transcend all of those "ego-state" limits, however briefly. "Yes, I feel my writing has grown or I have, or both – perhaps you can't have one without the other," a student wrote to me recently. Her observation underlines what I too have long observed: that breaching those limits *is* transformational, for the writer as well as for the writing. I sometimes wonder whether the traditional shape of the short story and the novel in our culture, in which a character moves toward epiphany or transformation, might be a translation into content of this fact – whether, in other words, the writing tends to mirror the process the writer her- or himself is going through. You're trying to go somewhere you don't know. And once you go there, you find out what you know.

However, this can never happen if you don't first commit yourself to turning toward the energy you feel and into the teeth of that unknowing, rather than turning away.

Writing Experience

FREEFALL WRITING

For now, write with a specific (internal) emphasis on discovering what, for you, has energy on any given day. If you can't find it, then "go fearward": write something that you find yourself especially reluctant to write about.

Writing Tip: Remember that not everything you write has to be shared with anyone. Releasing yourself from the obligation to do so may free you to write something you'd rather nobody else saw. But having done so, give yourself a chance to reconsider. Sometimes the act of writing about a particular subject or in a particular style eliminates the sense of taboo with which it began. If you do decide to show it to a writing partner, you may want to warn him or her that this is a particularly sensitive area, or to place some limits around how you want it to be discussed.

TIMED WRITING

Make a list of specific subjects which are difficult for you, but which you wouldn't mind being "forced" to write about for 15 minutes. If you're writing with a partner, you could either compare lists and see if there's any overlap, or agree to write at the same time about different subjects. Arrive at eight topics (each or shared), and write about two of them each week, for 15 minutes each. If you find you'd like to spend longer, extend it to 20. If any of these subjects comes up for you again during the week in your Freefall Writing, you may discover that you have yet more writing to do to explore it fully.

Writing Tip: If you find that the writing flattens out as you proceed, that's probably happening for one of two reasons: either the topic has no energy for you (even though you may have thought it would) or you may be getting close to something that has a great deal of energy for you (I think of the familiar cartoon situation in which the characters are tiptoeing around the ramparts of a castle, and saying, "Is it too quiet around here?" while huge monsters look down on them from above). Keep writing, and see what happens. Only you can tell the difference between the two situations. Doing the writing will help you to begin to recognise which is which.

Chapter Seven
Life, Writing, and the Ten-Year Rule

As you experiment further with this way of writing, you may well be learning – even without noticing it – to handle a considerable amount of emotional complexity. As I mentioned in the first chapter, when I worked as an editor I read many carefully designed and constructed stories that seemed to function, in the end, rather like a box of toys, with simplified characters taking part in simplified encounters, in worlds that lacked the sort of subtlety and richness we take for granted in everyday life. The problem, as I see it, is that the thinking, intending mind *does* simplify. It analyses and predicts, and plans accordingly, and the result – unless the writer can lose him- or herself in the writing despite the plan – necessarily lacks the intricacy and diversity of our daily experience. (That is probably why novelist Timothy Findley once wrote to me, "Working to a format is death!"[29])

But when people begin to write what has energy for them instead, immersing themselves – as often as not – in their sense of how something "really did" happen in their own lives, a wholly different capacity of mind seems to be engaged. In that kind of writing, a life-like degree of complexity seems to be a given from the outset – probably because it has never occurred to the writer to write in any other way.

However, writing about life – *using* autobiographical material (when it "comes up") to learn to write – does raise certain issues that don't otherwise come up for writers. In this chapter, therefore, I would like to discuss some of those issues, including the implications of the fifth precept, the so-called ten-year rule.

Autobiography Or Fiction – A False Dichotomy?

Historically, there has been a strong dividing line between writers who claim that autobiographical material can be useful in writing fiction and those who insist that it can't. Mario Vargas Llosa's well-known pronouncement that "[t]he real truth is one thing, and literary truth is another, and there is nothing more difficult than to want both truths to coincide,"[30] echoes those of Virginia Woolf and many others. Truth and fiction were "granite and rainbow"[31] Woolf insisted, "Let them meet and they destroy each other."[32] Others, however, claim to have discovered otherwise:

> I felt liberated the day or the week – it didn't happen overnight – that I discovered that I did not have to invent my stories in the way that children make up fantastic tales (or become chronic liars), but that I could use all the stuff of real life, that my work itself then gained in power, that I felt writing become holy when I moved into real life when I wrote, instead of out of it.
>
> It turns out that the only truth I know without much doubt is the one that is the story of my life. I mean the emotional truths, the precise descriptions of my experience of womanhood. I do not mean by this the exact details, the locations, the statistics as such, or necessarily even the things that happened to me.[33]

To me, it seems unnecessary to take a stand on either side. Clearly, what works best for some writers is to find a line of entry via the imagination (whether or not they then go on to draw some of their material from life – as Woolf and Vargas Llosa most certainly did), and what works best for others is to find a starting-point in life, which they then submit to the power of their imagination. When we're talking about the process of writing, surely *whatever comes up*, whether it be the product of one's own experience or of sheer imagination, must be allowable as a starting-point. To insist that it be any other way is nonsense.

The Value of the Ten-Year Rule

While I would never, therefore, claim that what comes up when you write according to the precepts "should" be autobiographical, I do notice that about ninety percent of the time, that is what does come up. I also think it's quite fortunate when such material comes up, because it not only gives rise to vivid and compelling writing, but also teaches the writer, very quickly, some essential lessons in how to relate to what he or she is writing about.

However, it isn't enough that the material simply be autobiographical for some of these benefits to arise. It also seems to be necessary for the writer to have acquired a certain distance from what's being written about. Ten years' distance is a handy rule of thumb; certainly, a considerable period of time needs to have elapsed since whatever was experienced took place. Older material often seems to shape itself very readily into a self-consistent whole in writing, with recurrent images and symbols reverberating through it in a completely different way. It's "the garden going on without us"[34] – a place of wondrous new growth and flowering. With events from the more recent past, the writing is often much less effective, and I find I can't rely on the writer's skills evolving in quite the same way through writing it.

I've thought a great deal over the years about why older material works so well for a writer. My understanding of why this should be so is this: because what is being written about is autobiographical, but is also distant in time, the writer can readily identify with the self that took part in it, but is also willing to let that world be what it is – to step out of the way and simply witness what goes on there. Without the ego-involvement that more recent events would call for, he or she can sustain a state of mind that allows other kinds of associations to take place. It's not a matter of "What does this material mean about *me*?" in other words, but rather of an engaged but open-handed curiosity about what's going on there. And that state of mind is exactly what a writer needs to have with regard to his or her material, no matter where it comes from. It's the essential writing state.

In this curious and attentive state of mind (which some writers have likened to sleepwalking), the writer can enter that world and allow new things to happen that he or she wasn't consciously expecting. Symbols can arise and resonances play forward, even through pages that haven't been written yet. The whole experience of writing can come to seem quite magical, in ways that can't be explained by that writer's rational, egoic mind. But whether or not the writing experience has all those features, the writer whose material is autobiographical quickly gets the chance to experience being deeply involved with a character who is not (now) him- or herself, while at the same time holding an open awareness of the world in which that character is involved. He or she becomes familiar with what's involved in simultaneously participating in, and producing, the world that's being written about.

I can vividly recall sitting hunched over the keyboard late one night with my heart pounding, when the protagonist of a scene I was writing arrived home to find her rapist sitting in her living room. I felt acutely afraid on her behalf, but at the same time, I knew I had to keep typing in order to find out what happened. Before that, I don't think I had ever consciously realised quite what it meant to have a foot in both worlds in that way – or, really, quite how much fun it could be. Yet that kind of split attention is what fiction, memoir-writing, many other kinds of non-fiction and even poetry demand of us. And what I'm saying here is that through autobiographical material that is more than ten years old, writers get a wealth of experience in just how that kind of attention works, and how it feels.

Once again, this is a process that takes place very naturally and unselfconsciously as you follow the precepts, and for that reason I'm not sure how good an idea it is for me to put it into words. The most important thing, of course, is that you continue to write, without which none of this can happen. And that as you do so, you bear in mind the fifth precept: when it comes up, autobiographical material which is more than ten years old can teach you some important fundamentals of writing creatively, very quickly.

The Vividness – and Privacy – of Childhood

Most of the basic material a writer works with is acquired before the age of fifteen.

- Willa Cather

Since for most of us, the ten-year rule would open up a length of time stretching well beyond the years of childhood, I find it curious both how often writers do have material from childhood emerge to be written about, despite the variety of prohibitions they may feel about writing it, and how very vivid that writing often turns out to be.

Why it's so vivid is an intriguing question. Psychologists seem to agree that we acquire new sensory experience using the right side of the brain (if we're right-handed, that is; left-handed people's brains seem not to be so bi-cameral). Most of the sensuous detail that we gather about the world, we gather in childhood, using it as a basis from which we draw inferences, make associations and predict – using the left side of the brain – for the rest of our lives. Perhaps because of that, when the writing takes us to those early experiences, they can feel almost as fresh and resonant as they were when we had them the first time, and they retain those characteristics when we transmute them onto the page.

In addition, possibly because of the way the brain changes as it matures, feeling and thinking seem not to be as separate in childhood as they come to be for most of us later on. A thought emerges almost as a feeling, and vice-versa. Insofar as "fiction tries to reproduce the emotional impact of experience",[35] it could be that the highly felt, emotional way of experiencing the world in childhood lends itself particularly well to the work of fiction.

But very often, when material from those early years does arise, writers find they have some powerful self-censors to get past. The Dragon of Privacy seems to guard this material fiercely. In addition to declaring it too personal ("What if your mother/sister/children ever saw this?"), that censor frequently delivers the message that it's simply wrong, or bad, or shouldn't be known about, for some authoritative reason that the writer finds difficult to put aside.

To me, as the reader, these reasons show themselves to be

astonishingly various, and yet the upshot is the same: given that this is the case, the writer *can't possibly go ahead and write what's come up to be written about*. One student came to me in anguish about the gods and goddesses she could hear speaking to her as she wrote – surely, she said, if she wrote down what they said, people would know she was crazy. But when she was able to overcome that prohibition, she went on to write and publish an intriguing non-fiction book in which she quoted what those presences said to her, to great effect. People have told me that they felt they shouldn't write about their childhood because it was too privileged; others have believed the same thing because it was too poor. Too crazy, too cruel, too chaotic – even too joyful: the sheer inventiveness of the prohibitions alone is impressive. But it's clear to me that the writing is often particularly strong when the writer can put aside these powerful objections, even just "for the time being", and write.

This writer, for example, was convinced that she should never write the stories that arose from her childhood, because of what they would expose about her family's struggle with the living conditions they encountered in the Far North. Yet when she put that fear aside, she wrote this arresting scene:

"Do you want a piece of bread?"

I don't know – what does Mother say? She's not even noticing me.

"Do you want a piece of bread?"

I don't know – if I take it and eat it without permission, I'll be switched. My stomach growls. I hear it growling out loud. Seething inside with hunger. I had fish at breakfast – a nice pink trout fried in animal fat.

"Do you want a piece of bread?"

Fish isn't so filling. Bread would be nice for a change. I want the bread but I can't say so until I get Mother's nod. She's talking to someone.

Please look my way. Tell me, do I want a piece of bread?

He's putting it away. Tell me I can have the bread.

He ties a knot in the plastic bag – the plastic bag that holds the wonderful, beautiful white bread. He's walking away. Saliva gathers in my mouth and I swallow. Look my way, Mother. Look at me! Do I want the bread? Do I? The man – he's walking away. Mother. It's been so long since I've tasted bread. Mother!

She glances at me and nods. I can have some bread! I do want bread – I do.

I jump up from my sitting position. I can almost feel the texture of the bread as it rolls in my mouth – rolling around – mixing with my saliva – the whiteness clinging to my tongue. I rush after the man carrying the bread.

I run beside him. My legs taking two steps to his one.

"Offer me a slice of bread again," I think. "Offer me a slice again. I can accept it. I want bread."

He smiles as I run beside him. He swings the bread back and forth as he carries it. I follow the bread with my eyes, back and forth, back and forth, wishing I could ask for a piece but I can't. It's alright if he offers me a slice. Mother has said I can accept it. But I can't ask for it. That's not polite. I'll get switched.

Oh please just offer me one more time and I'll say yes.

We come to his tent and I watch as he throws the bread into his tent.

(Pat Bearclaw)[36]

It would be a shame, in my view, if a scene as immediate and compelling as this one had never been allowed to be written.

Moving from Fact to Fiction

E.M. Forster observed that the natural state of mind for a writer, while he or she composes, is a state of love.[37] Where better to start, then, it seems to me, than with the worlds and characters one loves already.

As you will probably know by this point from your own experience of writing, one of the responses that arise when such things do come up to write about is the desire to move even closer to them – to give moment-by-moment attention to the characters and the events they are involved in, and to flesh them out in dialogue and specific, sensuous detail. It's easy to see how that has happened, for instance, in this example:

He's shorter than I am. He cannot reach to the centre of the car's roof with his cloth.

From the other side I say, "I'll do that bit."

All my life my father has done things for me. He fixed up my bicycles, he fixed up my first cars. When Alex and I were renovating our flat a year ago he came down and helped with the painting. He communicates with people by telling them things. A conversation with him is not an exchange, it's like a series of lectures.

"You've got a good car here," he says. "Can't fault the Japanese on their cars. These new Australian models are junk. A bloke down the road, he goes to the bowls club where your Mum goes, he bought one of these. First thing, he took it over the road to the gas station, a self-serve place, and he's standing there with the hose in his hand pouring the stuff in and he watches as the gauge goes up past twenty dollars, past thirty, thirty five, forty and he's thinking, Christ these are big tanks, and it still isn't full, but he can smell the petrol so he opens the boot and it's swimming in the stuff. The bloody hose wasn't connected."

Dad pauses, waiting for me to react.

"What did he do?" I ask.

"Drove it back over the road and said, 'I'll have another one thanks. This one leaks.'"

He laughs and sprays water on the bits he has soaped.

The car is parked beside the garage on a paved area. The soapy water runs into a drain covered by a green cast-iron grill. Pine bark chips come neatly to the edge of the bricks.

"It's a funny thing Dad," I say. "But I don't feel I really know you all that well. I mean you're my father, but I don't feel we ever really talk."

He makes a noise which is an acknowledgement I have spoken but nothing more. He keeps on cleaning his side of the car. I wash mine in the thickening silence.

"Do you know what I'm talking about?" I ask. "I mean I know things about you, but I don't really know how you came to be that way. Like I know you vote Liberal but I don't really know why, and it seems important..."

I'm washing the bit between the wheels, the bottom of the doors, a long slightly curved pane of smooth metal, like an underbelly. I feel as if I'm running off at the mouth here, a familiar feeling when I'm around my father. I didn't mean to mention the Liberals, I was embarrassed, looking for an example of what I was talking about and it slipped out.

I feel like a child, as if he's in control and I'm the one with the too obvious emotions. Except I'm an adult now and it's no good him pretending big people don't have feelings because I know they do.

He still does not speak.

"It seems strange to me that I don't know you," I say. "I mean apart from

Gabriel, you're the closest living male to me."

I cannot even see him. He's bending down around the back wheel.

"I thought we might go out together sometime," I say. "We could go to a film together."

"That's a good idea," he says, standing up, the hose in his hand. He turns the nozzle and water pings against the paintwork. "Your mother and I like to go to the films in Sydney from time to time."

He says this as if he really didn't hear the personal nature of the invitation, the asking of him, by me.

"You want to put some polish on?" he says.

(Steven Lang)

Yet the truth is that no-one actually remembers the past in this kind of minute detail. Once you truly begin to pay close attention to dialogue, or to any kind of moment-by-moment continuity of action such as this writer has shown, you are forced to begin to invent as much as to remember. You allow yourself, that is to say, to stay open to what *would* have happened, and you become very well able to create whatever is needed along the way. That's why I consider "I don't remember" to be an editorial comment. Make up what you need, and you'll find yourself perfectly satisfied, in the end, with what you've invented.

As you continue to write in this way, the line between fact and fiction will become less and less important, until eventually it's gone. Whether you're inventing or remembering won't matter – the writing will feel just as authentic, both to you and to the reader. Ultimately, when you decide you need to invent something out of whole cloth, instead of feeling as if there's a precipice you have to jump off, you'll be able to recognise that it's something you've been doing all along, and simply extend the impulse. And in that way, you'll have accomplished easefully what might have been very hard to learn to do any other way.

Discussing the Writing as Writing

In order to get the most from using autobiographical writing in this way, it's also important that you be able to discuss it *as* writing – separate from your life or the life of your writing partner. I can remember being in a writing group once when one person said to another (about her writing), "That sounds just like your sense of humour!" And I thought, "But that's not fair. If this story were by Charles Dickens, they would never get to say that. He's been dead for a hundred years, so his writing would just be discussed as writing." What will be most beneficial to anyone whose writing you read is to give them the benefit of the same sort of separation between life and writing, even if you suspect that their writing is autobiographical. The following are some things it may be useful to bear in mind in such situations.

First of all, I find it important to remember that even though your partner's writing may in fact be autobiographical, as a reader you have *no way to know that for certain*. In order for it to serve its purpose in this process, you need to treat it simply as writing. Doing this will give you a language with which to discuss it, different from the language suited to, say, therapy or confession. Treated in this way, it becomes material that can help the writer learn all the skills of good writing. Treated in this way, autobiographical writing remains an excellent vehicle for learning the skills of surrender.

The fact that you've agreed to treat this material simply as writing has several implications. One of them is that if you're the writer, you need to keep silent. Saying "This really did happen" or "I made this all up" adds nothing to the piece. You've said what you have to say – on the page. Now your job is to keep silent, and take in the response. Another implication – this one for the reader – is that even if the writer uses the first person (saying, for example, "I" and "my mother"), to infer that any character in the piece you've read (or heard) is a) the author, b) the author's mother, or c) anyone else the author might ever have seen or known, is what literary critics call an "illicit assumption". You can't know that anything your partner writes about a mother has to do with his or her actual mother, even though you may have known the woman well, and she seemed to you to behave in exactly the ways described. In fact, the writer might have seen his mother completely differently from the way you did, in real life, and made *this* character up out of whole cloth.

One of my favourite illustrations of this truth comes from Lois

Hudson's short-story collection, *Reapers of the Dust*. In the preface, she describes her mother's response to a story she, Lois, once wrote, set in her hometown in North Dakota, about a red-headed Jewish schoolteacher from New York, who had to write a Christmas pageant for the children even though she had no idea of the story of Christmas herself. "I never realized you were in school the year we had that little red-headed teacher from New York," her mother said. "My teacher was a North Dakota native and I have no memories of any instructors, Jewish or red-headed, from New York," Hudson comments.[38]

The implication, for your discussion of someone else's writing, is that you *cannot* know what is autobiographical and what is not, even if you were in that place at the time. You need to stick scrupulously with what you have to say about the person's writing as writing: what has energy for you there, and (if possible) what you think it is about the way it is written that makes that so. Don't wander off topic into your own inferences about the writer's life, even if you are left with strong emotions and want to express, say, your sympathy. Otherwise, the writer may feel exposed, and stop writing. ("Oh, poor Angela," one writer – we'll call her Angela – told me someone had said to her after her piece was read out. She said that that comment had stopped her writing for weeks.) Stick with what you know: what's working for you in the piece. And tell the writer more about that.

Writing Experience

FREEFALL WRITING

Decide that you won't ignore any impulse that arises to write autobiographical material. While you're writing, especially if the events you're writing about happened recently, stay open to any images or memories from further back in the past that might arise as you do so, and turn to them instead. Move in as close as you can to the events being written about, and give moment-by-moment detail, even if you're only able to do so for a few sentences at a time.

If nothing autobiographical does arise, move in as close as you can to whatever does come up, and give moment-by-moment detail.

Writing Tip: Whenever you can't recall a specific detail, reach for one that would have been possible and use that instead.

TIMED WRITING

Write for 15 minutes on each of the following topics, going to a specific scene whenever possible:

1. A road trip
2. Royal beatings
3. Bad doll
4. Unfair!
5. Running away
6. Lost treasure
7. A trade
8. Scarred for life

Writing Tip: Include as much dialogue in these scenes as possible.

Chapter Eight
The Dragons at the Gate

And the parched ground shall become a pool, and the thirsty land
springs of water: in the habitation of dragons, where each lay, shall be
grass with reeds and rushes.

- Isaiah 35:7

By now, you've begun the serious business of writing regularly. And whatever superego figures kept you safe in the past by not allowing you to write very much – or perhaps at all – may very well be redoubling their efforts to save you, now that you *are* writing. Those efforts usually manifest in messages from your Inner Critic, beamed at you more or less regularly as you work. The fact that writing in this way is often enjoyable and absorbing helps enormously in distracting you from those messages, but at some point it's also a good idea to turn toward them – to get to know those criticisms better, lest at any point you mistake them for the truth. In order to help you do that, this section will take a closer look at those Dragons at the Gate – the voices that seek to bar you from risking yourself in the light of the real world, so that you may rest forever in the safety of the shadows of what might have been.

The Dragon of Bad Writing

But as he scratched out as many lines as he wrote in, the sum of them was often, at the end of the year, rather less than at the beginning, and it looked as if in the process of writing the poem would be completely unwritten.

- Virginia Woolf, *Orlando*

Your very best help in dealing with the pervasive and persuasive shapeshifter who warns you about your "bad writing" is, of course, the second precept: "Don't change anything". But even if you're managing not to give in to the temptation to "unwrite" what you've written, chances are you are telling yourself some unflattering things about your writing. Now is the time to pay a little closer attention to those negative comments and decide what, if anything, you need to do about them.

I've found that for myself, one important decision has been to pay no attention to them whatsoever *on the day of the writing*. One of the most surprising discoveries I've made in writing daily is how regularly the despair I may feel about what I've written on any particular day gives way, often by the very next day, to modest approval, and a sort of bewilderment as to *why* it looked so bad to me at the time I wrote it. "It's fine," I realise, "It's the next thing." Or I may even find myself thinking, "That's not bad. I like that!"

So what happened on the day I wrote it? What I've come to see is that on that first day, when what I've written down on the page is still surrounded by all the directions I didn't go in and the things I didn't say, the contrast between what's there and what somehow might have been there is almost unbearable. But by the next day or the day after, when those other possibilities have receded and all I'm left with is what I've actually written, it looks fine to me: it carries the story forward, and a whole network of other possibilities opens up from there. If I had tried to change it on the day I wrote it, when I was so painfully vulnerable to this particular dragon, those pages and ultimately the whole project could easily have vapourised under its breath of fire.

What the Dragon of Bad Writing has to say about your writing in general is probably slightly different from what it might say to you immediately after you've written something, when you're in a state of newness and vulnerability. In general, it usually has several favourite comments that it's found can snag you, so you hear those repeated over and over in your head. I think it's well worth getting to know those judgments intimately, so that when they come up, they don't take you by surprise. (You can welcome them with a thought like, "All right, I know that's what you think. Off you go now," and keep on writing.)

One interesting way of getting to know them better is this: write down five negative things you often think about your writing. Having made that list, circle the one that has the most energy for you.

Now, for ten minutes, write as exaggeratedly *in that way* as you can. If the Dragon is muttering that your writing is too academic, for instance, write some extremely academic prose. If it says you're boring, be achingly tedious. Simplistic? Be very, very simple. Then have a look back, and see how it went.

Here are some examples of what I mean. In the first, the writer circled the message that his writing was "Too Heady", and wrote:

I want to make it clear that the person writing this is an educated person – at least has been schooled, and is articulate, thorough, and out of touch with his feelings. In fact, what are feelings? And we might consider the whole question, not just of feelings and their epistemological (or is it ontological?) status, but also what constitutes this much addressed topic, "sensuous detail". The advantaging of the sensory and proprioceptive, non-intellectual approaches to writing has led to a general decline, not only in literature but also in public life, and the expectations of what is considered legitimate and attractive in discourse generally. I myself prefer a more formal, thought out, and intelligently argued style that people think about. Being absorbed in passing visceral urges, the residues of emotional states, indiscriminate references to bodily hungers, is bordering – for a person of true sensibility – on the abhorrent and unpleasant. There is no advancing of the human agenda by lapsing into the underworld of the sentiments. They do not help the defence of the realm nor the advancement of commerce or the laws and institutions of the state. I prefer the language of the corporate prospectus or act of parliament.
(Harrison Malcolm)

Another writer, who found she had been telling herself that her writing was "Self-Indulgent Pap", indulged herself thus:

"It was the birds and their auroric song that roused me from the slumber of my dream. I thought I had spent the night meditating but I must have swooned in that midnight darkness, giving way to the dark mystery of sleep so that I could shed my old self and rise a new woman, free from a past that held me like bound feet. The birds called me forth even as I called them forth, and the sun sparkled on the waters of the lake beyond my window, spreading the diamonds of my new self so that I might pick the best of me and leave the rest to sleep on undisturbed. I would be new every morning and when I went forth, it would be with my light." Emmeline sank back into the satin pillows on her bed and smiled across the room at her best friend, Sandra. *"You see,"* she continued, *"I will bring only the best of me forward."*

"But Emmeline," protested Sandra, *"I like all of you! Even the not so good parts. They're all of you."* Sandra's eyes were moist with defeated passion.

Emmeline looked across the bed at her, smiled indulgently and said, *"You may have the 'all' of me that you like. But the world will only have my glowing goodness. For the world I will be diamond hard and brilliant and unbreakable. But you will keep the secret that is me: the opalescent, twilight parts of me."* She leaned over and kissed Sandra on her now damp cheek.
(Gloria Jean Bubba)

And even a writer who had been thinking of himself as unable to write at all found he had plenty of energy to write on this topic:

Blocked

Considering where I am at the present moment, somewhat weighted down by problems and in the throes of some slight nervous encumbrance of what one sometimes sees termed, at least in the tabloids and by writers of what we used to call "penny-dreadfuls", writer's block.... If you feel by any remote chance that that preceding sentence was too lengthy, in short overstretched and far-reaching by the nature of the number of words - that is verbs, nouns, adjectives etc. - it contained, and that you have therefore been unable to make cogent sense of it and have in general failed to join the subject with the main verb and thereby lost its general thrust, that is almost certainly due to the fact that you are not nearly as well educated as I am, and indeed may not possess the requisite amount of abstruse words not to mention prolix sentences.

Therefore, let me make myself clear. Considering where I am at the present moment, as I said earlier, it would be as well to consider the facts weighing upon the case in question. For it is only by this kind of careful, indeed deeply thought-out, deeply sensitive and highly skilled therapeutic investigation that any light at all can be shed on the aforementioned problem. This kind of slight mental disturbance, what we might term today as mild depression or, in the vernacular, being hacked off, pissed off or (regrettably) fucked up is not a new concept in the annals of Western culture. Indeed the Greek philosopher Pythagoras, who originated in the island of Samos and who is well known to every properly educated English schoolboy, was the first to discover it.

(Bruce McAlpine)

Only the time limit brought this last one to a halt, which gave a nicely ironic twist to the subject in question. But whether your foray into trying to do what the Inner Critic so facilely accuses you of doing results in a humourous piece of "showing", as in the above examples, or shows you how difficult you would actually find it to write that way, or simply gives you a few minutes to indulge your "plodding", "clichéd" (or whatever) proclivities, there's no doubt that you'll emerge from this exercise with a defused sense of the horror of writing that way, and the Dragon of Bad Writing will have lost some of its power to distract you.

Since the messages about your Bad Writing tend to change over time, it's not a bad idea to repeat this exercise occasionally. You'll always find it interesting and often, oddly invigorating.

The Dragon of Privacy

One of the critical voices that can't be quite so summarily dealt with is the voice we touched on in the previous chapter – the one that says, "This is too personal. No-one should know this about [name of friend or family member]" or, "I could never publish this." Throughout literary history people have worried about that voice; the Brontës, as is well known, agonised about disgracing their father and published pseudonymously, as did George Eliot and many others. Then, as now, the spectre of having people recognise themselves in their books, even if they *weren't* being represented there, has seemed to some writers unbearable. And even though our private lives have become infinitely less private than at any other time in the forefront of history, probably everyone who writes (except Isabel Allende, who claims that everyone who knows her has to know that she will use anything that comes her way in her writing, if she needs to) still worries at some time or other about whether people will be hurt by what he or she has written.

I take this concern seriously: there are people who probably would be hurt if they saw the writing you're doing right now – if you're writing everything that occurs to you to write, that is. But this concern has nothing to do with the present. It is a concern about what could happen in the future, and as such, it really is just another face of the Internal Critic. The Dragon of Privacy shows up frequently in this process, because so much of the writing that comes up tends to be autobiographical. But *in the present*, that's just another way of keeping you from becoming fully absorbed in what you're writing.

If you do find, however, that thoughts about what might eventually happen to this writing, or who might see it someday, are too distracting to be put aside, then consider this. None of the writing you are doing right now may end up in anything remotely like its current form, should it ever evolve into a short story, poem, essay, or other finished product. When Alice Munro, whose short stories often sound highly autobiographical (even when they aren't), was asked how much of her work was based on reality, she said, "Reality is the starter-dough"[39] – an image that I find a memorable reminder. The grey lump of starter is unrecognisable in the tawny, shining, finished loaf of bread, even though without it, that loaf could never have risen.

But above all, what's important to remember right now is that you are engaged in a writing *process*. For that process to work as it must, for you to learn to follow your own energy in writing, and come to trust writing as an activity that will bring to you what you could not have foreseen, you need to allow yourself to be fully vulnerable to *whatever* comes up to be written. Of course you may not be able to show everything you write to anyone. And sometimes, when you do show it to someone, and you can see from their response how very well it's working, it may feel painful *not* to be able to try to publish it. But once again, those eventualities are for now, mirages of the future.

So for now, it is crucial that you stop allowing this particular Dragon to have your attention, and write what's there to be written. If you deprive yourself of the experience of entering fully into what has energy for you today, you will never even know what process of transformation would have taken place – in you *or* in your writing – before it eventually saw the light of day.

The Dragon of Unworthiness

Many people have a voice inside that tells them they can't even aspire to write. It's too lofty an ambition, or too audacious. And in that way the Dragon of Unworthiness can retreat to its lair, unchallenged.

My guess is that that particular voice gets its power from an almost exclusive acquaintance with published writing – as if no-one ever wrote anything that hadn't been published first. Once, when I had only written a few scenes from the first draft of my first novel, I was told I would have to give a reading alongside several very well-established writers. I agonised over that for weeks, until I realised this: I was going to be showing something very young to people, something that, compared to the other people's work, was still in its infancy. But no-one ever looks at a baby and asks it why it isn't an adult. They say, "What a lovely baby." I realised that I could say without apology where I was in the process, and read those scenes without feeling the least bit ashamed. The whole experience, which was richly rewarding, shed new light for me on the value of *all* of the stages of writing. Anyone, I realised, could say, "My writing's in its infancy; it hasn't reached the stage of publication yet," and still feel justifiably proud.

The Dragon of Unworthiness has some other guises that are worth noting, so that you can recognise them as such, should they come up. "Laziness" is one of them. Just not getting around to writing is often self-described as "laziness", when in fact it is the result of someone's struggle with the conviction that they can't or shouldn't do what they're about to do, such that they therefore (rather wisely) put off trying. Labelling yourself as "lazy" is one way out of a hopeless situation. But writing, even in the face of this particular Dragon, is another. Over time, it really will get tired of breathing fire and return to its lair.

Another is Disorganisation. If you don't value your writing enough to keep it safely organised, then Unworthiness has the upper hand here, too. You cannot, by definition, see the larger picture of which *all* of your writing is a part. Do you remember the example I gave in Chapter Two of John Guare coming across a vital link for his play in a letter he had written? The conclusion he drew from that particular incident was, "Keep everything, because this is the great fact. We are all strangers to ourselves."[40] Don't let an ego-problem, in other words, subvert the larger process that your ego doesn't even comprehend. Preserve your writing, on faith, from the Dragon of Unworthiness.

The Dragon of Not Being Publishable

The conviction that the kind of thing you're writing is not something that anyone would ever want to publish is yet another way, in my view, that people use to take themselves out of the "now" of writing. Your job for now is to write, and to keep concerns about the future from impinging on the process.

To worry about whether the end result of what you're writing will be what someone else wants is analogous to trying solve a problem at the level of the problem. Before you're finished, your work will take several quantum leaps that you can't at the moment even imagine. And even if you could guess, your notions of what would sell and what wouldn't could only hamper you, as Edmund White points out in an essay in his collection, *The Burning Library:*

> *Part of my problem as a young writer was that I was too much a New Yorker, always second-guessing the "market". I became so discouraged that I decided to write something that would please me alone – that became my sole criterion. And that was when I wrote* Forgetting Elena, *the first novel I got published. In my courses later I always forbade my writing students to discuss in class the commercial side of publishing. I wanted to save them the time I'd lost; I wanted them to be serious artists free of all constraints.*[41]

So when this particular Dragon rears its head, tell yourself, "I'm free to do what comes to me, here." You are in a process of developing and getting to know yourself as a writer, and there's never been a writer quite like you before. Don't let that precious process of discovery be compromised by mere ambition.

The Dragon of Being Publishable

Something that's come up for a number of my students is the sudden surge of fear, now that they're about to be published, about having people read their work. It's usually touched off by what someone else who knows their writing says to them: "You're going to feel so exposed" or "Surely you're going to publish under a pseudonym." That transition from the secluded world of writing to exposure to public scrutiny is often a painful one. But it is true that once someone's memoir or highly autobiographical fiction is about to be published, the time really has come to confront the fear of exposing others.

While most literary agencies and publishing houses have in-house lawyers who will go over the work with you from a legal standpoint, or suggest people who can, that may not be as important to you as how family members or friends may react. If that is the case, then you have several choices. You may want to show it to them first, and get their reaction (which can often strike the writer in you as weirdly beside the point, but important to the relationship nonetheless). You can consider publishing under a pseudonym. Or, you can decide to go ahead and publish it anyway, and deal with the fallout as it comes. I'll never forget one of my students looking up at me through her hair, tears still in her eyes from her initial reaction to a fellow-writer's warning, and saying with a small smile, "I think he underestimates my strength." It made me think of Florida Scott-Maxwell's statement, in *The Measure of My Days*: "You need only claim the events of your life to make yourself yours. When you fully possess all you have been and done, which may take some time, you are fierce with reality."[42] It seemed clear to me that with that small smile, that writer had taken just taken a giant step toward becoming "fierce with reality". Watch closely to see whether there's a part of you that would like to do the same.

The Dragon of Writer's Block

While I'm not sure if anyone reading these pages finds it hard to write *at all*, perhaps the dreaded Dragon of Writer's Block still deserves some attention. What is it really, this extended state of non-writing that we hear so much about? Is it any more than a (very painful) fixed idea?

Here is a description of this situation that any writer might find useful, should it arise, because so much information is packed into so few words: the "dead-end of narcissistic despair known as writer's block [is one] in which vanity and guilt have so persecuted craft and imagination and so deprived them of their allies – heart, curiosity and will – that they have gone into exile and into the sanctuary of silence."[43]

It seems to me very possible that all writing is, in a certain sense, a form of narcissism. Narcissus, of course, was the young, handsome god who fell in love with his own reflection, kissed the pool in which he saw it, and drowned. He's certainly had a bad rap in psychology over the years, but he was also a very lovely, young, male energy – almost the prototype of the kind of energy in us that is active, lively, passionate, and actually puts something out there. I don't think there would be much writing to be read if people didn't want other people looking at or at least *with* them – if they weren't saying, "Look at how I see it. This is what I see." Indeed, I often wonder whether in the early development of most artists, there hasn't been some sort of mirroring defect – not enough of the kind of reflecting back from parents that some psychologists[44] claim is so important to a child's development.

The reward is a glorious sense of accomplishment when it all goes well – people do look, and they *do* see, and the ego can feed from that, even if more fleetingly than one might have imagined. But that passionate dependence on a shared vision can also flip over all too readily into its opposite, making the writer morbidly vulnerable to the opinion of others, and therefore much too ready to judge him- or herself negatively in order to pre-empt scrutiny. Because of that, the fear of negative judgment can cycle in on itself, in what the description I quoted above calls a "dead-end": no-one else is ever going to get a chance to look, the writer decides. You can't make me do this at all.

This stubborn, rather rubbery Dragon can be surprisingly tenacious. But the fact is, sometimes you do have to write through sheer terror –

the terror of what seems like certain failure. An intelligent, supportive writing friend or small group can be of great help in breaking that deadlock, by looking at what you *are* able to produce (which may not be particularly wonderful at first) with insight and compassion.

I also find it helpful to remember that in nature, nothing stays the same: perpetual change is one of the basic laws of existence. So if this state has persisted for very long, you're accomplishing something that's not natural. At some level, you must be willing it. Examine its purpose (which is probably in some way or other to keep you safe). Now consider whether you can achieve that purpose in any other way and begin to do so, freeing yourself to write.

Writing Experience

FREEFALL WRITING

As you continue to write according to the precepts, allow yourself to witness what the Inner Critic is telling you about your writing. Note down those messages in your writing journal. Twice this month, do the exercise suggested in the text of this section: make a list of five of those comments, choose the one that has the most energy for you, and write for ten minutes as exaggeratedly in that (suggested) style as possible. Read the result to your writing partner if you have one. And remember, sometimes this exercise produces funny or illuminating results; sometimes it doesn't. Either way, it's worth doing.

Writing Tip: For the purposes of this exercise, it's best to re-phrase inner critical comments that come with a negative qualifier, as in "not enough x" or "not x enough", because they're harder to show. Thus, "not interesting enough" would need to become "boring", "not enough depth" would work better as "superficial", and so on.

TIMED WRITING

Write for 10 minutes on each of the following topics:

1. Making a mistake
2. How could you?
3. Don't let me down
4. Just do it over
5. That isn't funny
6. Trying to win
7. If only …
8. Cheaters never prosper

Writing Tip: Let the topic take you into a specific incident or scene. Don't stay above it, musing "about" the topic. (This is a repeat from Chapter Three, just in case you need it.)

Chapter Nine
A Writer's Discipline

Despite discovering how absorbing it can be to write in this way, and despite learning to recognise and face down some of the Dragons that keep you from it, you may still not find that you turn to writing gladly. For almost all of the writers I've ever known, the act of writing involves some sort of inner struggle. It doesn't really seem to matter what they do – have a project they love to work on, find a good mentor, attend an inspiring workshop, or publish a novel to critical acclaim – putting words down on the page still demands some effort of will. It seems as if the very risk involved in creating something out of nothing arouses some resistance with which the writer must find a relationship in order to work at all.

In an e-mail written a few weeks after a workshop, one writer gave a vivid description of how that struggle felt to her:

After I arrived home, everything that I thought I had gained at the workshop seemed to disappear, and I once again entered into drought. Sometimes I would sit at the computer, and feel frozen. Often I will be writing, and suddenly all energy seems to drain from the subject, and there seems to be nothing else that grabs me. So I write on through the aridness, and find that I can, in fact, keep going. Once I read a piece out to my partner, who to my surprise thought it was great. His respect for my bleats for time to write has gained ground. This brings up two thoughts: first is the difficulty in writing at home with the demands of work life and partner and family, and the second is that without feedback, I have no idea as to what is OK writing. I have been so shocked at losing it all again that I have not as yet been in touch with anyone else. Why does it have to be so fucking hard? It seems to me that writing is an essentially joyous process, but for me, obviously not. The book I felt would simply fall from my pen is a long way to being even started. However, I am determined to keep plodding along, even if it is not possible every day, I still aim for every day. And to trust the process to carry me through, as I ultimately do.

(Lea Weaver)

My experience with other writers supports my belief that if she keeps at it, she will do well. But I think that most of us, if we're honest, have many days when we find ourselves asking the same question this writer asks about writing: "Why does it have to be so f – ing hard?"

Often, as for this writer, no sooner has someone embraced the precepts and begun to find writing easier, than old habits of mind begin to re-assert themselves, and the very strengths of this process begin to look like liabilities. In the world of speed and product, joy in the freedom to write "what comes up", for instance, can soon be vitiated by a sense of impatience and pointlessness. Relief that the Inner Critic (some of whose Dragons I described in the previous chapter) has finally retreated far enough to make writing possible can leave you open to a new fear: the fear that now, "I have no idea as to what is OK writing." And if events from the past are what is coming up in the writing, the headlong sense of discovery can give way to the lurking suspicion that you are not the narrator at all, but that past self all over again – as if, as Malte Laurids Brigge, the Rilke character whom I quoted in Chapter Six, puts it, "it is just as difficult as it used to be, and [...] growing older has served no purpose at all."[45] "If I cannot come to terms with myself over past issues, and they come up," the woman quoted above wrote in another letter, "I founder and get stuck. How can anybody who may read my writing forgive me, and not judge me as I judge myself? How can I even think about them and face them for myself?"

Beset by such fears and uncertainties, a writer can all too easily decide that, for today, it's better not even to try. A day goes past, and another, and another, and pretty soon that steadily writing self is only a memory. A very valuable and precious one, stored away to be brought out and dusted off at some easier time in the future, but no longer a day to day reality to be lived among the uncertainties and difficulties of the present.

So how to continue – given the tenacious hold of habit on our lives – to write? At this point in the process, something else is needed. Something that simply holds up a hand to all the busyness, overwhelm, panic, procrastination – *whatever* guise the impulse not to write may appear in on any given day, and says, "No." Something that says, "I will write today. No matter what."

What follows is an anatomy of the "something else" that's needed – something that I call "a writer's discipline".

The Only Useful Definition

For people who have spent much time in psychotherapy, "discipline" has become a bit of a dirty word – and rightly so, I think. It commonly seems to imply some imperious directive on the part of the superego that forces all the rest of who we are to do its bidding: "You will do this because I say so!" That's something most of us have worked far too long and hard to *stop* doing, to be willing to start up all over again. It used to be that before I could get the word "discipline" out of my mouth, I'd be struggling with a "you can't make me" that had far more power to resist than I had will to subdue it. Ultimately, my conclusion was, "Well, if that's what I have to do in order to get some writing done, it's not worth it. There has to be some other way."

That other way was revealed to me when I came across a definition of discipline attributed to Carl Jung, which I found revolutionary: *"Discipline is the obedience to awareness."* Discipline is not, in other words, a matter of bending one's will to some ruthless injunction, or of engaging in a form of abusive inner warfare, but rather a process of staying focused on something one already knows to be true, and allowing oneself to do whatever is implied by that knowing. We come

107

to writing because we already know that we want or need to write. We didn't ask for that knowing: it's *a priori*. It's a given. So discipline means that we pay attention to that awareness, and do what is implicit in it. We write. My own experience is that no matter how much hand-wringing I may put around the act of writing, there is also a (sometimes very subtle) sense of peace that emanates from the fact of actually doing it. It has a quality quite apart from the eternal busyness of the rest of what goes on in my mind. It seems to touch and to be born from a deeper place than that. My job is to remain aware of and connected with that deeper place. My job is to write.

I was amused to read Natalie Goldberg's description of coming full circle with her Zen master's early injunction to her to write, which had informed so much of her life from that time forward. As she mentioned in the introduction to *Writing Down the Bones*, he had once said to her, "Why do you come to sit meditation? Why don't you make writing your practice? If you go deep enough in writing, it will take you everyplace."[46] Building on his conviction, she did make writing her practice, producing several books along the way and becoming well known for having written about making writing the centre of her life. In *Wild Mind*, she recounts the story of asking him, late in his life, "Why did you say so many years ago that I should make writing my practice?" And his answer: "Because you like to write. That's why."[47] Maybe it's never any more complicated than that. Or any less. What he was saying, in effect, was that she already had the awareness; it didn't come from him. Because he suggested that she obey that awareness, she made it her discipline to do so. But in fact, both the awareness and the means to obey it were already present within her from the start.

That's one of the reasons, I think, why people find coming to workshops so helpful. The workshops, like the precepts, are designed to help writers serve their own awareness. They've given themselves that period of time. They've given themselves over to someone who knows how to help them protect and marshal that time. And so the writing blossoms. If they go home and it wilts again, does that mean that going to the workshop was somehow misguided? If you've tried the precepts and discovered how well they work, but you're not writing, does that mean that you or the precepts are wrong? You already know that it doesn't. All that's missing is the permission to make that awareness matter. And it is in giving yourself this permission that the discipline of writing comes in.

An Anatomy of Discipline

Since few of us have a Zen master to tell us what we already know, it's worth examining further what actually constitutes "obedience" to our own awareness from day to day. When we hold up a hand to the chaos and say "No. I will live according to my awareness today", what is that going to look like? What happens next?

In my experience, obedience to our awareness of the need to write doesn't look any different from living out of a deeper awareness in any other aspect of life. One of the most cogent and succinct descriptions of the bare bones of that kind of orientation I know comes from Angeles Arrien, a Basque writer who has listed what she sees as the four basic requirements for sitting in sacred circle – another profound, in this case communal, way of attending to a deeper awareness. They are simply to show up, pay attention, tell the truth, and remain unattached to the outcome.[48] Examined more closely, they constitute as good a breakdown as any of the kind of discipline that's called for in the writing process as well.

1. Show up
Any number of writers, including Hemingway, have been credited with the statement that the one true necessity for a writer is to "apply the seat of the pants to the seat of the chair". And any number have said that they find they need to "pretty much do that" every day, as Stephen King claims he has done, "whether the work went well or the work went badly".[49] Walter Mosley is emphatic: "If you want to be a writer, you have to write every day. The consistency, the monotony, the certainty, all vagaries and passions are covered by this daily reoccurrence."[50] Why? Because in his experience "writing a novel is gathering smoke"[51] and we live in a world where:

Reality fights against your dreams. It tries to deny creation and change. The world wants you to be someone known, someone with solid ideas, not blowing smoke. Given a day, reality will begin to scatter your notions; given two days, it will drive them off.[52]

To him, it doesn't matter how long you write each day; as long as "[y]ou have re-entered the dream of the work", that's "enough to keep the story alive for the next twenty-four hours".[53]

But what about writing in the way I'm talking about here, in which each day – or each half hour – may bring a new story? Is there the same need to "show up" every day, in order to keep that process alive? All I can tell you is that for the people who do it steadily, one insight leads to another, and the process unfolds in a more or less unbroken progression into a genre, be it fiction, poetry, memoir, or other non-fiction. I frankly don't think it's realistic to expect yourself to do anything every single day and still have a responsive, spontaneous approach to life. If you miss a day or more, the ability quietly to return to the writing without berating or giving up on yourself seems to be an asset. But the truth is that as with any other activity, when you've done it often enough, regularly enough, you begin to want to do it. Finally, you're working *with* the force of habit, rather than against it. And maybe that's a break we all deserve to give ourselves. To show up. Starting now.

2. Pay attention

I've found over the years that in addition to "showing up" physically, I also need to be willing to show up mentally – in other words, to pay attention. No sooner had I discovered how to put words down on the page without excoriating myself, than I discovered another layer of resistance which translated into making notes when I sat down, instead of writing. It almost felt as if I were a plane coming in to land and I couldn't put my wheels down. They'd touch down for a phrase or two every now and again, and then I was in the air again and spinning, scrambling down notes against some future time when I would write this out properly. I now know that showing up means arriving fully on the page, or "choos[ing] to be present" as Arrien says.[54] It's not a matter of telling myself that I can change it all at some time in the future; it's a matter of putting one word down after another in the now, meaning them, and leaving them there. Writers are not just inventive on the page; they're endlessly inventive, it seems, at finding ways of avoiding getting to the page in the first place.

Only you will know how long you need to pay attention *for* each day. The important thing is that you really write – and you know when you're writing. It has its own unique quality of presence. "Pay attention to what has heart and meaning,"[55] says Arrien of sitting in a circle, listening within. Allow yourself to be fully present for what you connect with most deeply in writing. Pay attention. And write.

3. Tell the truth

What she means by this, I believe, is exactly the same thing I mean by going where the energy is, and writing what's there, without shying away from it. And when there seems to be nothing in sight that has any energy? Or when "suddenly all energy seems to drain from the subject, and there seems to be nothing else that grabs me," as the student whose letter I quoted above discovered? Her response is the only one possible: "So I write on through the aridness, and find that I can, in fact, keep going." She's still obeying, in that moment, her awareness of the deep, *a priori* connection with writing that exists for her, despite the apparent lack of something to write about in that moment. Thus all the time, under whatever circumstances arise, she is staying as close as possible to the truth of what's there for her. And in so doing, she continues to cultivate the essential witness state of writing. Arid and dry are superficial and transitory. But the act of writing, so practised, remains constant and deep.

4. Don't be attached to the outcome

Perhaps the hardest thing about this way of writing (and yet the most necessary for anyone who practises it to learn) is to bear in mind, always, that it is a process. Once you begin to see any one thing you're writing as a product ("I will use this for x" or "I can publish this in y"), you begin to lose the power and the freedom of its forward movement, the way one piece of writing builds upon another. Before long, thoughts of the outcome begin to influence what you say as you go along, and you (often unconsciously) begin to put severe limits around what can happen in your writing.

To be attached either positively ("I can use this!") *or* negatively ("I'll never be able to use this!") stops that otherwise inevitable progress. Trust that there will come a time when you can go back over this work and, if you like, see what's usable for some other purpose. Believe that when you do, you will be looking at it from a very different perspective than is available to you now. And for the time being, just write.

Writing Experience

FREEFALL WRITING

Write every day for two weeks, without missing a day. As always, bear in mind the five precepts and, for this two-week period, consciously recall Angeles Arrien's advice to show up, pay attention, tell the truth, and remain unattached to the outcome.

Writing Tip: Keep daily notes in your writing journal about how that daily practice feels to you, and what you see happening in the writing as a result of it.

TIMED WRITING

Write for fifteen minutes on each of the following topics (the first two are good to write with someone else, even if you don't have a regular writing partner). Although the first two may inspire a more general overview, remember to let the others take you to a specific scene or situation.

1. Why do I write?
2. What stops me?
3. Making a change
4. "Change back!"
5. No show
6. "Do you want to know the truth?"
7. What if?
8. After that, nothing was the same

Writing Tip: Keeping track of how your writing goes for you in your writing journal can be an invaluable aid in developing the witness. It also gives you immediate insight into the way the writing state changes from day to day. In that way, you can quickly see the folly of becoming attached to any one image in the whole kaleidoscope.

Chapter Ten
A Poet's Way of Mind

The grand power of poetry [...] is its power of so dealing with things as to awaken in us a wonderfully full, new, and intimate sense of them and of our relations with them.
- Matthew Arnold, *Essays in Criticism*

Perhaps because my own inclination is to write prose, the majority of people I work with seem spontaneously to produce work that heads off in a direction recognisably like that of fiction, memoir, or some other creative form of non-fiction. But what if your writing just doesn't go that way? What if you're following all the precepts and yet, day after day, the writing refuses to run to remembered or imagined scenes, or to expand into any kind of longer, more sustained narrative? It's possible, of course, that one of the Dragons is blocking your path, and you will have to keep working with it in order to find a way forward. But another possibility – the one I would like to address in this chapter – is that you have a fundamentally poetic turn of mind. For poets, this kind of surrendered writing can work in a very different way.

It goes without saying that no-one needs to make a *conscious* choice between poetry and prose unless he or she wants to. Numerous writers

115

create both, and do so beautifully. But the writers I'm talking about here don't seem to have the option of making a conscious choice. From the first, in their writing, it looks very much as if the choice has already been made for them.

For example, in response to "A Sound Heard in Childhood", that timed writing exercise I often give on the first night of a workshop, the majority of writers will be taken by a remembered sound into some scene or incident. But for one writer, what emerged was this:

Sometimes I can hear the sound of warm tin, like a tulip folded around pebbles. Ticottle, ticottle, they scatter around banging the thick sweaty goats fur, echoing the boulders and clods of dried mud on the sides of the mountains. I bet their hoofs clatter and slip, ticottle, spinata, dung dung, ticottle.

(Marie-Elsa Bragg)

Instead of moving forward, her mind spontaneously circles, returning to let the sound of the goats' bells spin off new sentences. This piece is short, but it's instantly evocative – and to me, immediately recognisable as the writing of someone whose natural inclination is poetic.

Have a look at the writing that follows, written by someone whose mind circles in a similar way, and who works herself into frustration on three separate attempts by thinking it should be otherwise.

I might have been Salome dancing far from home. I might have been the Queen of Sheba craving the green Nile scent of apples, the taste of falling rain, telling Solomon goodbye to return to my own people. I could have been a woman of the Harem destined to breathe air behind a curtain of black veil rather than the free and fresh air I breathe. I could have been some scribe taking down the words of Rumi as he twirled and spun into a golden ball of light throwing off incandescent sparks. How to transcribe those? I could have been a junco with a black capped head. But I am right now a writer whose fingers have not found much today, although they stayed at their stations of the keys with persistence. Today I did not fall, I barely walked. I had to settle for crawling slowly.

The next day, she begins:

My mother's legs at eighty-one remained as shapely as a waltz. The rhythmic turn of calf. The quick pause and glide to ankle. She could have been a dancer with those legs, a Ginger Rogers twirling with Fred. Or, a Spanish dancer with a red flounced skirt and black shoes that stamped the floor and upset the heart beats of the crowd. She could have been a pin-up girl like Betty Grable. I don't know if she ever danced. I know she had a blue flapper style dress worn for some festive occasion [...] I don't think my mother was vain about her legs. Not like me. I lamented and cursed the heart surgeon who mined for a vein in her leg and left a zig-zag scar racing up one leg. A sweatshop seamstress would have done a neater and less obtrusive job. So she could have danced across the stage of heaven in a blue dress and seamless legs.

And finally:

Oh, darling fern frond. Oh, burly leaf of blackberry. Oh, ivy that chokes and overruns. Oh rhododendron blossom sagging and wilting after the ball. Oh spotted fawns living in a city yard, how will you believe the woods should be your home. The sun is playing hard to get, shyly or coyly hiding behind the curtain of clouds. Oh, death where is thy sting? My finder fingers are lost in the alphabet woods. They turn this way and that. Each path leads somewhere. Some of them loop back and intersect. Some of them lead to the Emerald City, some of them are dead end and require the pathtaker to double back, to retrace the steps already taken until reoriented.

Not only does her mind circle around a central image, it extends that image not by means of a series of causal links (as in a story), but by a series of substitutions: this is (like) this, like this, like this.

When this writer tried to do otherwise, each attempt ended in frustration. Finally, she concluded:

My Freefall Agent does not take directions. He/she/it is listening to a different drummer, one I can't hear. I am lost in the alphabet soup, swimming with p's and q's (what are p's and q's?), buying vowels, selling a few on the open market for petty cash – just enough to buy lifesavers and coffee beans. So maybe I should issue different orders or let it play.
(Susan J. Erickson)

117

If your own writing is emerging in a similar way, or you're interested in the minds of people for whom it does, you may be interested in exploring the nature and implications of what I've called a "poetic" way of mind a little further. That could make it easier for you to do what this writer discovered she must do, and did successfully thereafter: to listen to the drummer you *do* dance to, and to "let it play".

The Primacy of the Image

The most prominent characteristic I see in writing of the kind I've just quoted is a sense of what one group of early 20th century poets called "the primacy of the image". Whereas many prose-writers seem to turn up incident after incident in their writing right from the start, Erickson's sentences are peppered with arresting sensuous images: the "green Nile scent of apples", the "taste of falling rain", the "quick pause and glide to the ankle", the "burly leaf of blackberry" – and bereft of incident overall.

Equally striking is her gift for metaphor (which plays on sameness and difference in such a way that the thing being described, which I.A. Richards called the "tenor" of the metaphor, blazes anew in our minds: cloudiness, when it's paired with coyness; the alphabet with woods; legs with a waltz, for instance), and for extending those metaphors. No sooner is the "tenor" paired with an image (which Richards called the "vehicle" of the metaphor), than the image itself begins to take on a life of its own. Of writing: "Today I did not fall, I barely walked. I had to settle for crawling slowly." "The sun is playing hard to get, shyly or coyly hiding behind the curtain of clouds." "My finder fingers are lost in the alphabet woods. They turn this way and that. Each path leads somewhere. Some of them loop back and intersect. Some of them lead to the Emerald City, some of them are dead end and require the pathtaker to double back, to retrace the steps already taken until reoriented." And then of course there's what happens to the superb comparison of the shapeliness of the mother's legs to a waltz ("My mother's legs at eighty-one remained as shapely as a waltz. The rhythmic turn of calf. The quick pause and glide to ankle" and all that follows from there). Even the word-plays that arise equally spontaneously hinge on the same kind of penchant for pairing sameness with difference: "finder-fingers", "seamless legs", "stations of the keys".

In all of these examples, the ability to grasp an image anew seems to take precedence, taking on a life and a generative power quite unlike the generative power of incident or story. Perhaps it's not too much to say that the primacy of image over incident here may signal a truly basic difference in way of mind.

The Power of Substitution

By and large, poetic power seems to have not only to do with seizing (or creating) the most telling image, but also with making it tell – making it stand for other things.

In other words, a poet's power is to a great degree the power of substitution. "For all the history of grief," says Archibald MacLeish, in his poem, *Ars Poetica*, "An empty doorway and a maple leaf."[56] Metaphor, that essential leap of mind whereby one thing becomes another, and an empty doorway can stand for grief, is one kind of substitution. Word-play, as we have noticed above ("finder fingers", etc.) is another. Symbolism, in which one term stands for a whole network of relations, is another.

The Russian Formalist critic Roman Jakobson claims as his own a valuable discovery which seems to me highly relevant here. Working with people who had stroke-induced aphasia, he discovered that their language difficulties fell into two distinct categories.[57] One group displayed what he called a "metonymic" or associative disorder. They tended to mix words up in a way that was based on the association of things in space, time or through causation: "chair", they might say for "table", or "bang" for "gun" (a chair is often near a table in space; a gun causes a bang). The other group of aphasics appeared to suffer from a quite different sort of word-confusion based on substitution: "black", they might say, when they were trying to say "death", or "snake" for "danger". This he called "metaphoric" disorder. His conclusion was that metonymy and metaphor are fundamentally different linguistic acts which stem from two different parts of the brain. Could it be, then, that differences in our very brains are a possible reason why some people seem naturally to come up with writing in which "poetic" acts of substitution take precedence, while for others causation or "letting one thing lead to another" seems a much more spontaneous way of proceeding?

Of course, the fact that some people's predominant way of writing is metaphoric doesn't mean they can't write narrative, and those of us for whom narrative predominates can and often do write poetry. We can all name poets who went on to write highly successful fiction, and prose-writers who also write poetry. Even if the difference in brain functions is as clear-cut as Jakobson would have it be, what I see in people's writing is a continuum, with people who, like Erickson, find it hard at first to do anything but substitution at one end, and people who do little that could ever be described as poetic at the other. Most writers fall somewhere in between.

Showing vs. Telling in Poetry

By this point in your experience of following the precepts, you will probably – if your inclination lies in the direction of prose – have discovered already how much more effective "showing" is than "telling" in bringing you present in your writing. The right scene, heartfully chosen, really does take you inside a situation far more readily than the proverbial thousand words. The immediate, sensuous details seem to jump past the intellect and take you straight into the world you're writing about, in a way that no abstract concept or general summary ever can.

Not surprisingly, the same holds true for poetry. Abstract, general words that summarise whole series of situations (a word like "love" for example) seem to keep you thinking, whereas when you can give a sensuous image that "shows" love, both you and your reader can be taken into the immediacy of the experience. (T. S. Eliot, as you may recall, coined the phrase "objective correlative" to describe exactly that – the way an image or a configuration of images works to give the reader precisely the feeling that the poet was trying to convey when he or she wrote it.)

What follows is an excellent demonstration of the power of "showing" in poetry. As a timed writing exercise with one group, I gave the abstract word, "Stupid". Aline Burke, whose writing falls well toward the "poetic" end of the continuum, wrote the following:

Stupid

> *My sisters are older*
> *And I am too small*
>
> *How do they get into those books?*
>
> *I cannot make the letter A.*
> *I cannot remember what goes together*
> *Or why a red apple held up in the blue morning*
> *sky*
> *Looks like what A seems to mean.*
>
> *Why am I not as much a fact*
> *As two and two*
> *Equals the forever four?*

I can't think how anyone could have conveyed the meaning of the word "stupid" more succinctly than by using these images: the red apple of the spelling primers against the blue morning sky, or the first bald ultimatum of the arithmetic book: 2 + 2 = "the forever" 4. Working as much with the connotations of these images as with the meanings of the words themselves, this writer makes us feel in an instant what "stupid" means to the younger sister: too young, too ignorant, too unable to connect, and throughout it all, heart-wrenchingly, doomed to be left out.

It's important to note here that I don't think she achieved this feat by thinking, intellectually, about what images would best convey these concepts. What this writer did was what she had experience in doing through following the precepts: *she entered into the perspective of that character* and let that perspective call up the images that made their way into this spontaneous poem. Once writers have begun to learn fully to inhabit the worlds of their characters (and/or past selves) in this way, they can follow those characters' perspectives in the direction of either prose or poetry. Here, simply and evocatively, this writer has made use of this small child's perspective to write a very effective poem.

Freefall Writing and Poetry

Writing in an open, spontaneous way with the precepts as your guide provides an excellent way to condition the poetic reflex – if you can allow it to do that for you. Just as Burke was able to enter the perspective of a small child experiencing herself as "stupid" in order to discover the images that comprised her poem, so you may also have had the experience by now of entering into other perspectives in your own writing. One of the liberating things about this way of writing for many writers is that it can take them back at least some of the time to childhood when, as we've discussed, the way in which images fell upon the mind felt fresh and new, and alive with connections – in other words, when the metaphoric power was high. My hunch is that anything you've written from the perspective of childhood will be full of potentially poetic imagery – *if* you found yourself able to allow it to be.

You can look back and see metaphoric power at work in a number of the examples of writing based in childhood in previous chapters – and, I suspect, in your own writing, too. But it's nakedly clear in the following piece, also written by Aline Burke, which shows the small child actively reaching for the similes and metaphors that can express in words what she sees. Like the example with which I began this chapter, this was also timed writing based on the topic, "A Sound Heard in Childhood":

Putt, putt, putt, putt, putt, putt.
The motor boats have left the collars. The rowboats are anchored where the fishermen switched vessels. I watch from mine and my sisters' bedroom. It is dawn. The water is grey-blue, calm. You can see the slow drifting clouds on the surface. As the boats go out the putt, putt fades. Small wakes fan out in the clear water like opening zippers that dissipate into the great stillness of the calm liquid skin. There are six boats altogether. The Letempliers with Uncle Francis, the Lavallies, with Paul the mayor and Cletus who is on welfare. There is Gordon with Roderick and Fred. The last boat is Old

Lawrence whose presence reassures everyone and his two youngest – Danny who is just starting at twelve and Conrad who is eighteen.

None of them swim.

I worry a minute then leave them in God's hands. I crawl back into bed between Madonna and Roseann. I wonder how to make words of dawn that is steel blue with a blush of pink that opens to the fishermen like a shell and makes a silence so deep inside men that I want more than anything to speak of dawn and fishermen and motorboats and water fans.

I am warm between my sisters like a puppy in its litter deep and safe in its den.

Good is morning with the beach like a necklace between deep places inside and out. Every room carries the whole round far different minds deep inside my family's heads.

There are no words for this.

My sisters breaths are like the soft mood of the ocean washing in a circle of ins and outs.

Rose has a whisper of a whistle as she sleeps as the rose colours deepen and the sun climbs its way to another day.

I can't hear the putt, putt. The men are so far gone. Soon the ocean will be on fire with the glare of a full red sun. Soon I will forget this stillness, the dogs are waking, one by one their howls rise up. Good is morning Rose ann, rose light. Madonna, my family, all come through night.

Soon we will be day time as ordinary gravel and dust as it rises from the road.

Soon we will fight about who will dry the dishes and who gets the crust on Mom's loaves of bread. Soon nothing will be deep and silent until it is time to come back to bed and board the long dark phantoms with stars the only guarantee.

Unless it is too dark for even them to be seen.

One of the things I love in this piece of writing, and that I think is worth pointing out to those of us who find too little in the way of imagery coming up in our own writing, is the fact that the writer doesn't rush to coherence. She's willing to let an image emerge half-way: "Small wakes fan out in the clear water like opening zippers that dissipate into the great stillness of the calm liquid skin," for example, and, "Soon we will be day time as ordinary gravel and dust as it rises from the road." Or to let a half-formed incantation arise: "Good is morning Rose ann, rose light. Madonna, my family, all come through night." The result is writing with the potential to be put to use, someday, for either poem or story. The images and the story are both well begun here; they have only to be extended.

It's also worth noticing that here, as in the earlier piece on the sound of the goats' bells, the power of story actually exerts very little pull. The writer enters through the mood of a moment in this character's life, and she lets that mood sustain her. From the moment she hears the "putt, putt, putt" of the motors at dawn, she stays within that character and looks – exploring all that's to be experienced there, without the rope of a story to pull her along.

My advice, then, if you lean toward what I've described as poetic writing, or if you would like your prose to be enriched through the means of poetry, is to let your "Freefall Master" play more, play longer, and see what comes up for you. Don't be too quick to turn to the old, familiar patterns of narrative to save you. In the meantime, watch for the signs: the resonant images, the symbols that don't settle, the substitutions half-made that may yet prove to be powerful. And if you find that your writing is rich with all these things spontaneously, don't fight it or try to force yourself to tell a story. You may already be a poet in the making.

Writing Experience

FREEFALL WRITING

For the next several sessions, allow your writing to spread out from a particular remembered mood, or feeling. Be specific, as always – a particular day, a particular mood on that day. But rather than allowing yourself to be pulled away too fast by an event that unfolds on that day, let the writing extend that mood. Concretise the feeling in what the person sees, hears, tastes, and touches in his or her surroundings. And allow their mood to pull in whatever images may come up as the writing proceeds.

Writing Tip: Whatever mood you find yourself in over the next few weeks, see if you can "ride it down" to an entirely different time and place, in your writing. In this way, the roller-coaster of changing emotions we typically experience can, if we let it, provide access to a good deal of otherwise inaccessible material.

TIMED WRITING

1. Do a ten-minute timed writing exercise showing the sensuous images brought up by each of the following more abstract words: (choose 5)

   a) hate

   b) soul

   c) stubborn

   d) awkward

   e) unwanted

   f) alone

   g) guilty

   h) calm

2. Look back over your Freefall Writing and see what some of your pieces seem to be about. Find a noun that would sum up what the story is about (desire, loss, envy, disillusionment, for instance). Take that word as your topic, and for ten minutes, give the concrete, sensuous images that come to you in connection with that word.

3. Look back over some of the dialogue you've written, and see if you can give a single physical action on each character's part that would sum up what he or she has said.

4. Have fun with some metaphors via the following list, pairing each item with another thing:

> The sun is ...
> My heart is ...
> My big toe is ...
> Your voice is ...
> My hope is ...

Make up your own list, and do some more.

5. List the settings from five of your Freefall pieces. From each setting, choose a central image (if it's a desert, "the sun" perhaps) and create a metaphor with that image ("the sun is ..."). If "the sun is an axeman"(for instance), walk that image through your story: "The heat cuts my legs out from under me", "sun splits open the crown of my head", etc. (things that an axeman might do). Get the picture? If you do, you've grasped the principle of the extended metaphor. Take it away!

Writing Tip: With whatever objects you see around you for the next few weeks, ask yourself, what is that like? What could that stand for?

Chapter Eleven
Letting Go; Sinking In

As John Gardner memorably observed about writing, "if the effect of the dream is to be powerful, the dream must probably be vivid and continuous."[58] To me, the most important thing for your writing at this stage is that you maintain the closest possible relationship with the world you're writing about – that you dream it vividly, and sustain that dream in such a way that you can learn as much as it has to teach you about writing while you do that.

Much of what I have been exploring with you up to this point has had to do, either directly or indirectly, with helping you to stay immersed in what you're writing. Each of the five precepts – writing without forethought, not changing anything, giving sensuous detail, following what has energy for you, and allowing enough time to pass so that the ego is willing to let go of the material – plays a role in helping you to maintain your absorption in whatever's come up for you to write about. "Showing" it rather than standing outside and "telling" it is yet a further way of deepening this immediacy. And becoming familiar enough with your own characteristic patterns as a writer (the Dragons at the Gate, your own discipline, and your natural bent in writing) that you don't subvert that absorption is also crucial.

Here and in the next two chapters, I'd like to take a closer look at some choices you can make that will deepen that immersion: three techniques that will help the writing move beyond your conscious control and take on a life of its own.

But first, I want to address what may have begun to feel to you like a more immediate question: how do you remain "surrendered" – open to what comes up, spontaneous and uncensorious about how you write – and yet make a choice to use a "technique" such as I'm about to suggest, at the same time? How do you remain "surrendered", in other words, and yet bring in intention?

The answer to that question lies with you. If you've already done many weeks of writing in the way I've been suggesting, you may find nothing disturbing in making some choices *as* you write. You may find that choices that would have interrupted the flow for you earlier on, now help to deepen the process. But if any of the suggestions I make from now on seem to threaten the spontaneity of your writing, ignore them for now. This way of learning to write unfolds in its own time, and most of what I'm about to suggest will eventually come about in your writing anyway. (To check: take a look at the writing exercises suggested at the end of the previous chapter. If those suggestions, which purposely involve bringing some conscious intention to the writing, strike you as confusing or threatening, don't complicate the process in any way right now. Just continue to write.)

. It's worth noticing, however, that during this whole process of learning to surrender in writing, you have been bringing some intention – albeit unobtrusively – into the mix. Writing coherently and following the precepts has required some degree of willing and intending, as has "showing" rather than just summarising. By degrees, you will find you're able to bring in more intention. What's of critical importance here is not to let it get the better of the balance.

Letting Go of the Narrator's Control

A paradox in writing that I touched on in the chapter about "showing" is that the more you try to let the narrator (which for practical purposes we can equate with you, now, telling the story) control what goes on in whatever world has come up for you to write about, the less able that world is to take on a life of its own. But for a variety of reasons, getting that interfering narrator to bow out is not always easy to do. It's hard to trust, at first, that whatever you want the scene to show will be shown if you just stay close to the experiencing character (or past self) who's *in* the scene and let it unfold. And even if you already know from experience that you don't have to keep interrupting the scene to comment or explain, you can find that you're reluctant just to stay with the character and not pull away to comment, especially if the material is challenging. But if you can stay in the perspective of the main character and *not* step away, the dream of the work often deepens and the lessons it has to teach you about writing become more profound.

I think you'll begin to see what I mean by comparing these two pieces of writing:

Now, long after the dance career, she stares at her feet in the bath and recalls her very first ballet class in the Ketchum Hall, near Jesse Ketchum school in Toronto, a class taught by Betty Oliphant, the tall young teacher just arrived from England who had succeeded her first teacher at this location. (The first teacher had taught a rather free, so-called "Greek" dancing – really more "perch and run" than anything else, but she had loved it.) She arrived at her first real ballet class in navy bloomers and navy knee socks from her school uniform. Everyone else was wearing pink tights, black leotards and leather ballet shoes. She was mortified, but she stood at the barre as she was told to. "Stand like a princess," said the tall teacher with the kindly grey eyes. (She came to adore this teacher, and to be willing to do anything for her.) And so it began, her long obsession with the world of ballet.
(Jocelyn Allen)

The subject is the girl's "very first ballet class". And what we can glimpse of it – her standing at the barre, mortified in her navy bloomers and knee socks, makes me, anyway, want to see more. But that's difficult to do, because the narrator keeps cutting in. That narrator needs to tell us about her previous class ("really more 'perch and run' than anything else") and what happened later ("She came to adore this teacher, and to be willing to do anything for her"), and we're never really allowed to settle into the girl's experience there.

When that narrator can stay back, despite the temptation to comment from her own point of view, it suddenly becomes much more possible to see what that girl sees, and feel what she feels. Here, she and her mother are shopping for pointe shoes:

The girl sat down and pulled on the first pair. "Very tight," she thought to herself, but Bernadette commented that they had to be tight. As all pointe shoes, they were hardened in the toes with layers of glue and paper and covered with pink satin. There was a short barre attached to the store wall, and she held onto it and went up on her toes for the very first time. She was on pointe! What a thrill! "Hmm, those look about right," said Bernadette, and grudgingly, "Nice feet." The girl's feet encased in these hardened, tight pointe shoes hurt a lot, but she would never have admitted it. "Let's try the other size on, just to be sure," said Bernadette, the saleswoman. The girl reluctantly came back to earth, pulled off the size 5 shoes, and pulled on a slightly bigger and more comfortable size. "No, those are too big," said Bernadette. "See how the satin is bunching up at your heel?" Bernadette was the expert, and she, the student, was the novice. She and her mother accepted the verdict. They took the smaller tighter pointe shoes, my mother paying the $20 [today about $80!], and clambered back down the dented stairs to the street, the girl clutching the brown paper bag with its treasure of pointe shoes, pink satin ribbon (gros grain on one side so as not to slip), and pink darning cotton.

Now we (and the writer) are free to experience this world, with its treasures and its tight shoes, more vividly. We can catch a whiff of that older narrator (she's the one who knows what "all pointe shoes" are like, and what they would cost today), but as an interrupting, commenting presence, she's no longer in our or her own way. Now it becomes possible for the scene to take its own direction – and I think (somehow the "dented stairs" make me feel) that it's about to.

Letting Go of the Narrator's Agenda

Sometimes – especially in non-fiction – it's difficult for writers to let go of a narrator (or a character aligned with the narrator) who represents their agenda in a scene. Yet interestingly, once they can release that agenda and just sink into the immediacy of what their character sees and experiences, the very insights that gave rise to it can come across in a whole new way.

In this first piece of writing, the narrator urgently wants us to see all that she sees in the scene, but she's so much in the foreground that we can hardly see around her:

What I really want to write about is the sheer bloody awfulness of Moradabad and the people working there like in the bowels of hell [...]

Alam greeted me with an open, unlined face and a gentle, knowing smile. He wiped his hand on his dhoti, looked at it and held it out for me to shake. His forehead was smooth and he crouched down in the dirt in front of a pile of fine black sand. Next to him, a small fiery hole in the floor held a crucible of molten brass. A sooty curtain hung just beyond the furnace. It moved and two children laughed pushing it aside to see what was going on. Alam looked over and smiled softly at them. I looked and I saw squalor and craftsmanship and kindness and contentment and poverty and National Geographic brown-eyed brown skinned chiaroscuro beauty, brown, black, turquoise, flaking paint and shining hair, fiery metal and glinting brass. I felt like a voyeur. I felt like a pornographer. I felt like a thief, an overblown beached whale of a white woman, grossly privileged, not knowing I was even born. I wanted to take photographs. I wanted to paint the scene. It was the colours of a Caravaggio. It was the end of the line for Western consumerism. It was this man's life. It was his tradition. He called one of his children over to work a small hand bellows powered by a bicycle wheel set in a groove in the ground near to the furnace.

"Is there anything that would really improve the quality of your life?" I asked, feeling like the Queen, or worse, the Duke of Edinburgh.
(Chris Seeley)

But when she can let go of the agenda she began with (to show "the sheer bloody awfulness of Moradabad and the people working there like in the bowels of hell" and how different it is from life in the West) and instead show exactly what the I-character actually sees, a completely different aspect of the scene takes over:

I followed his gaze and saw a young girl crouching down in the dirt. She was wearing a faded dress with pink flowers on it and puff sleeves. She looked up at me with her white teeth showing. I smiled back. Next to her on the floor I saw a pile of brass platters. They were the kind of thing you wouldn't actually want to eat food off, but might be presented from one businessman to another, engraved to commemorate some great meeting. The filigree edging of the unfinished casting glinted sharply in the light.

Alam was a small man who moved easily around his workspace without ever really standing up or sitting down. His legs looked flexible and strong as he leaned back on his haunches with one elbow resting on his knee. He brushed his hands together lightly to clean off that black sand. I could see a few hairs on his chest poking above his cotton vest. He had a full moustache and thinning hair brushed over his chestnut scalp. The light hit the left side of his face strongly, leaving the right side in darkness and playing over the contours of his features in a gradual shift between the light and the dark. He had clear almond eyes, with dark irises smudging into creamy whiteness. His eyes had long eyelashes that curled outwards. His forehead was smooth and he smiled a relaxed smile, looking up at me openly. His teeth were the same pale cream as the whites of his eyes.

He picked up the mould he was making the plates in and undid a metal catch, releasing the fine sand and tipping it into a pile on the floor by his feet. Leaning forward now, his hands moved deftly and he worked at a steady pace. His eyes didn't need to look at what his hands were doing as he crumbled and reworked the sand for later use.

There was a small residue of cast brass in the neck of the mould which he had broken off the latest casting. He [shook?]out this "y" shaped piece of metal clattering into a tray and, with some of the sand, he passed it out into the alleyway through an open wooden entrance. Turquoise paint peeled off the panelled wood. It was the kind of paint finish interior designers might take an age to recreate.

Outside, two boys took the tray into the sunlight and began to sort fragments of brass from the sand like they were panning for gold. When they'd finished they passed the sand and then the metal back to Alam. He blended the sand into the pile in front of him and put the metal pieces into the crucible. He nodded at one of the children, who picked up the crucible with long metal tongs and lowered it through the hole into the furnace under the floor. Alam took a finished platter and began to make a fresh sand mould for the next casting.

With this clearer sense of being embedded in the I-character's immediate experience, rather than in what she and the narrator might think about what she sees, I'm able to step through the earlier, "National Geographic" image of human labour and into the essential dignity and complexity of the life of one human being. I have the sense now of its wholeness: of the parts played by family, economy, experience and tradition, so that in an important way, for the piece as a whole, the balance has shifted from voyeurism to participation. If the I-character were now to ask, "Is there anything that would really improve the quality of your life?" I would be better equipped to accept the question and more ready, I think, to understand his answer. As overwhelming as the whole task of conveying this scene clearly seemed to this writer in the first version, here she has carried it out deftly, by letting go of the ideas behind it and staying with the immediate experience of the character.

Letting Go and Letting Them Talk

A highly useful tool for helping you to stop trying to over-control the narrative is dialogue. When you begin to write dialogue, the kind of spontaneous unfolding that takes place in a scene can be astonishing. It's as if the characters stop being simply pawns in *your* story and begin to control their own destiny, once you let them speak.

This fact is demonstrated quite clearly, to me, by what happens in the following piece of writing. In the first piece, the narrator has a high degree of control over what we can and cannot see, and she moves through the tale of her character's first experience of summer camp at speed:

Soon the trunks arrived. All the trunks but mine.

"Well," said Robin, "I'm sure it's here somewhere. It probably got over into one of the other cabins or maybe it got sent over to the boys camp."

Oh God, I hope it didn't get over to the boys camp. What if they open it and see my underwear? I'd have to never come out of the cabin the whole summer. They would see my name on it and they would know what my underwear looked like. My stomach began to ache. I sat on my well-made bed and watched the other girls unpack their trunks, finding cubbies next to each other the way they had found beds. So much excitement as one girl brought out her new bathing suit and cap with the rubber flowers on it and several others cooed in mock jealousy. I had a pretty bathing cap too, with pink and blue rubber flowers on the side of it. I wondered if I'd ever see it again.

And so the evening passed, then a day and another night. I slept in my shorts and t-shirt. The counselors brought me a new set of navy blue shorts and a tee shirt with a swan on it, floating in a pool of water with the words, Camp Swan Lake under the pond. The blue lettering on the tee shirt matched the color of my shorts. I was also given a toothbrush and paste to put in my bathroom cubby. By the end of the week, when it was laundry day, I had no laundry bag at the end of my bed like the other girls and virtually no clothing to send out. I was afraid I would never see it again if I sent it out. I began to wonder if this was how things were going to be for me the rest of summer. Perhaps they had stopped noticing that I only had two pairs of shorts and two tee shirts. I began to feel sick all of the time. I couldn't eat and I cried myself to sleep as I heard giggles and whispers all around me with an occasional reprimand from Robin or Sharon.

"All right girls, that's quite enough. Flashlights off now."
(Cathy Henschel-McGerry)

But watch what happens, both to the story itself and to the pervasive sense of an intervening narrator, when she goes back to explore the "evening [that] passed", with the intention of allowing in more dialogue:

At about 5:30 in the evening, my cabin mates and I walked the five minute journey to the mess hall. I walked behind, but still close enough to hear two girls, each of whom wore white shorts and an oversized, navy Swan Lake tee shirt from last summer. They each had white socks with flowers around the ankles and white sneakers.

"I wonder if Kevin Moss is back this summer."

"God, he is so cute. I think I won't be able to eat if I see him."

"I know what you mean. You know I think he might be a CIT this year."

"Last summer, he came up to me on the last day and ruffled my hair while he told me to be good."

"Oh my God, you never told me in your letters."

"I know. I didn't wash my hair for three days. But by the time I actually wrote you, school had started and then we moved."

"Oh my God, don't look, don't look, but Steve Hawkins is over there picking his nose!"

"Oh gross me out. He's such a pig. I can't believe he is here again."

I tripped on a stone as I was straining to hear what they were saying. They seemed to know what was going on here and who was who. I fell and they turned, but when they saw me, they turned away and kept going.

"What's her problem?"

"Yeah really," I could hear them chirp as I brushed myself off, my face getting hot, my shame swelling. As we approached the massive building I heard a clamor of sound coming from within. I waited in line with my cabin mates to find our table. Each table looked the same: picnic style with benches. Each table was covered with a red and white checked plastic table cloth and had two ketchups, two mustards, two salt and pepper shakers and two plastic holders filled with white paper napkins. Each table set in rows spanning the entire lodge had silverware laid out surrounding a white, ceramic plate. The plates were scratched with years of use and washings.

As we made our way through the narrow rows to our table, the two girls who were not near enough for me to actually hear their conversation, were still deeply entrenched in it. Robin and Sharon took their places at either end of our long picnic table. I looked to them and the others for what to do. Everyone stood at his or her tables. No one sat. The girls turned away from the boys' side and began to giggle. They caught me being captivated by their seeming ease and comfort.

"What are you looking at?" one said, accusing me.

"Nothing," I said as I looked away, my cheeks beginning to burn.

Although I couldn't hear her words' lower volume as she spoke to her friend, I could see her mouth moving and make out what she said.

"What a geek!" Her friend nodded in agreement. The jury was in.

The director of the camp blew a whistle, which hung around his neck;
three short blasts which hurt my ears and got everyone's attention. The
tumultuous hall quieted. The shuffling of feet and benches, the clinking of
silverware and the admonishments from counselors to campers came to a
halt. The quiet ran through me like warm water in the tub.

"A hearty welcome to all of our campers. Are we going to have a great
summer?"

"Yeah!!" the room rocked.

"I can't hear you ..."

"Yeahhhh!!" I put my hands over my ears, as did many of the girls at my
table and the tables near us. Smiling and giggling spilled about the hall as he
held up his hand in mock understanding of what he could finally hear.

"Okay then, lets have a great dinner and then we'll do announcements."

As with the previous piece, it's as if another dimension has been
added to the scene, and we're now seeing it in 3D. More characters
than the I-character are now living and breathing, and a specific pair
of adversaries has turned up to thicken the plot. We're certainly forced
to wonder how suited this character would ever have turned out to
be, trunk or no trunk, for the camp experience. It's hard to forget that
arresting sentence, so redolent of home: "The quiet ran through me like
warm water in the tub."

The earlier control that the narrator had over the story, as well
as the speed at which the story moved, have had to be relinquished
in order to include dialogue and now, paradoxically, much more can
happen. Sometimes it feels more like a matter of standing by and taking
notes than of writing, once your characters are permitted to speak for
themselves.

Writing Experience

FREEFALL WRITING

Stay observant about what comes up for you, and go with some of the subjects that your mind shies away from. Stay with the perspective of the point of view character as she or he experiences the action of the story, as far as possible without moving outside that point of view to comment, fill in background, or explain.

But if that proves difficult, try entering a less challenging world for a while and staying *there*, making it your task for this period of writing to enter fully into the consciousness of the point of view character, and to stay there.

Remember to observe the other precepts.

Writing Tip: Make note of the times you feel compelled to break out of that character and of your reasons for doing so. Look back, and see if there are reasons that recur. If so, consider whether there are other ways you can accomplish what you need to do *without* stepping away from that character's point of view and experience.

TIMED WRITING

Write for fifteen minutes on each of the following:

1. Ashamed
2. In my element
3. Sink or swim
4. Stranger in a strange land
5. The death of a pet
6. Get used to it
7. Just superstition?

8. Shopping for happiness

Writing Tip: If it feels appropriate to where you are now in your writing, then as you write these pieces, jump into the perspective of the specific character (or past self) that comes up, and stay there. As in your Freefall Writing, don't comment, fill in background, or explain. Just see as much as the character can see, at the time that the character can see it. You won't need to go on doing this forever, but if you haven't yet had this experience, it may be time.

Chapter Twelve
Dialogue

In the previous chapter, I alluded to the fact that dialogue (otherwise known as direct or quoted speech) has a special magic all its own. Once you can begin to use it freely, you'll find it holds the key to much that would otherwise have remained locked away. Characters come into being for you with a new kind of immediacy and can begin to take their own direction, apparently much less encumbered by any designs you might have had for them. Their relationships emerge in new and unexpected ways, along with a host of unforeseen sensuous details. And with that new immediacy seems to come a lessening of the burden of being a narrator: there are other forces at play now that can allow the story to develop on its own. For all these reasons, it's worth spending some more time with this simple phenomenon: letting your characters talk to one another, and finding out from them what they have to say.

You'll have noticed, by the way, that when I say "character", I often follow that word with "or past self" in parentheses. I do that because for many people who come into writing this way, an earlier "I" – the person they were, say, ten, twenty or thirty years ago – is the main character in the writing that comes up. It's not always easy to recognise the fact that that former "I" *is* a different character from you, now, but nonetheless it is true. I vividly recall, when I was beginning to write a novel for which some of my own earlier experiences were the "starter-dough", complaining to a friend, "But I find the girl so *embarrassing.*" My friend said, "Well, she's you, pre-therapy, pre-meditation, much more uptight – of course she embarrasses you!" I realised when she said that, that not only was that girl's perspective different from mine now – her vocabulary was different, too. I was slipping into the perspective of someone who was *not me now* (something all fiction-writers need to be comfortable doing) – and I was already trying to back-pedal fast!

From then on, I could see how important it is to honour a past self's claim to being a character, if only so that you can let that character do what it wants to do and not interfere. None of this is to say that autobiography is the same thing as fiction. But it *is* to say that truly entering the viewpoint of a past self in writing is excellent training for seeing through the eyes of *any* character.

In this chapter, I want to explore the value of having those characters, whomever they're based on, talk to one another.

Listening In

One of the exercises I sometimes ask people to do is to find a café, preferably one where they can sit close to other diners. Their task is simply to write down what they hear. Obviously it's going to be hit and miss: sometimes you'll be able to record a nice, extended passage of conversation; sometimes you can only catch fragments and observe the way people drop their voices when they're about to say something really significant. But whatever happens, the writer in you can learn a great deal about the nature and rhythm of conversation by doing this, if you can set aside whatever reservations you may have about eavesdropping.

But the most important tool for writing natural-sounding dialogue comes from memory: from listening with the inner ear not just to the kinds of things the people who come up in your writing say, but also to *the way* they say them, so that as you hear, you can freely allow their voices to emerge on the page.

Sometimes it's necessary to use a timed writing exercise to get yourself to take the plunge into writing direct speech. ("The Same Old Argument" is one I find works well.) But individual writers often find their own ways of hearing the voices of the people who come up in their writing, quite spontaneously. Here's an interesting illustration of the way one writer worked her way inward to hear the voice of a woman who was to become central to her first book – her main character's stepmother, Kit. The process began when a small piece of that character's reported speech emerged in her writing:

Miss Burne [a teacher] *suggested I should go and read in my bedroom and I explained that although I had a bedroom of my own I was not allowed to go up there in the daytime.*

"Why not?"

"She says I wear out the stair carpet."

I had not considered this funny or unusual before. I had lived with Kit for fourteen years and I had got used to her ways.
(Laura Austen)

It was a voice that seemed impatient to be heard. She next reported, "I wrote a lot at breakneck speed. It may have been the first time I got Kit's voice down on paper." This is what she wrote:

"Why are you sitting there with your head in a book? For goodness sake get outside and do something."

"Don't come and ask me what there is to be done. You know perfectly well what needs doing. Go back up to the bathroom and clean the taps."

"You have a nasty nature. I have always told you that."

"You will never have any friends until you become a different kind of person. You don't deserve to have friends. You never will do."

"Why can't you be more like Carol? Everybody likes Carol. If only you could be more like her."

"You spoil everything. Why do you always have to spoil everything?"

"Take the piece of cake nearest to you. I can see you trying to take the biggest piece."

"As soon as I unwrap a sweet paper, you prick up your ears. Honestly!"

"Do you ever think about anyone but yourself? Do you ever think about me? I've given up my life for you."

"Come here this minute."

"If I've told you once I've told you a thousand times."

"If looks could kill, I'd be dead long ago."

"You are a liar. Why do you always have to tell lies? Can't you ever tell the truth?"

"Come here or I'll knock your block off."

"I only touched you. Why are you making such a fuss? Anyone would think I'd hurt you. You want to see what some children have to put up with. You just don't know when you're lucky."

"Don't let me ever hear you say that again."

"Why don't you make the best of yourself? You don't know what you look like in that. Go and look in the mirror. Just go and have a look at yourself. I wouldn't want to be seen dead like that."

"Why can't you be more grateful after all I've done for you? I've worked myself into the ground for you and that's all you can say. 'Sorry!' What good is 'Sorry'?"

"Get a move on can't you. For goodness sake go away and get out of my sight."

I may be imagining it, but it seems to me that the stepmother's voice becomes stronger as the piece goes on. I'd go so far as to say that even though this is just a list of her comments (in direct speech), a rudimentary plot shows signs of developing. As the narrator lets go of the kind of grip on the action that indirect speech ("She says I...") maintains, the conflict within the triangle implied here seems to escalate: between the scapegoat who knows that whichever way she turns she will be attacked; the good sister whose life and inner compromises we can only begin to imagine; and the stepmother herself, trapped in a decades-long regimen of taking care of a child she has chosen to despise.

Start listening now to the conversations around you, and to the voices of the characters in your mind. Make it a habit to jot down some of what you're hearing. That way, you won't hesitate to use dialogue in your writing the next time the opportunity arises – and it will definitely arise.

Dialogue is Physical

Direct speech also works to bring writers much more immediately into the physical presence of whatever it is they're conveying. I wonder if it's the fact that dialogue requires ears and a mouth (rather than just the presence of the mind, thinking) that calls forth what seems to be a much more heightened awareness of the presence of the body. Like a musician in performance rather than in rehearsal, a writer using dialogue seems to engage fully and directly with that moment with his or her whole being, rather than settling for a more distracted run-through of how it might go. "This is it," as Natalie Goldberg says of the present moment in writing, "Right here, whatever comes up."[59]

Watch what happens to the following piece of writing when the author of this piece (Janey Runci) shifts from what is basically an interior monologue to using direct speech:

(first version:)   *Two weeks after I went back to boarding school I had a letter from Father Dowden. He had finished the pamphlet story about the boy and his mother. He was working on another one. What did I think about a story where a group of teenagers went on a camp in the hills behind Wynyard? There would be a girl in it who found it difficult to mix with the group, but she would change during the time they were in the camp. I smoothed the pages out on my desk at night study and wrote back about the girl. Two weeks later another letter came, and after that it became a regular thing. Usually letters from anyone but our families were opened by the nuns, but because these letters were from a priest they were left untouched. I was allowed to seal my letters to Father Dowden before I gave them in for posting. On the nights when I had a letter to answer from him I raced through my homework and then I wrote and wrote and wrote.*

(second version:)   *I carried the letter in the pocket of my tunic. As the afternoon got warmer and we finished Maths and moved onto Geography my hand slipped down and fingered the folds of the paper. The Geography lesson was about the different kinds of vegetation found at different heights on a mountain. Sister Phillip had drawn a hill shape in a square on the blackboard before class. Now she ruled lines in white chalk with the large wooden ruler. "Copy this into your books, please, girls." She propped the ruler*

143

at the side of the blackboard and rubbed her hands together to get rid of the white chalk. "Neatly now. Make the square about six inches." She brought her fingers up to her face as if to inspect them. She began picking at the thumbnail on her right hand. It made a slight clicking sound.

I looked down at my page and began drawing the square. I drew in the hill.

Up at the blackboard Sister Phillip had coloured in the bottom stripe of the hill green. I lifted up my desk lid and held it propped open with my head. The smell of pencils and the banana I was going to eat after school was strong. I reached for the pencils but then I stopped. I wanted to get out the letter and open it now, read it again. My hand moved to my tunic pocket and I pulled the letter out. I spread it out inside the desk. It was hard to read but I could see the spidery writing and I knew the opening sentence.

"Dear Janey," I read, "I've finished the book, so thanks. And now I'm onto another one." "Got your pencils ready, girls?" Sister Phillip was tapping the ruler lightly on the green stripe when I lowered the desk lid.

"I'm onto another one," I said the words of the letter to myself. The new one was to be about a girl who went on a camp, a group camp in the hills beyond Wynyard.

"Imagine this is a mountain," Sister Phillip said. "Write at this point," she tapped the first line, "One thousand feet."

I entered the numbers and saw in my mind the curved shape of a hill behind Wynyard where we'd been on a family picnic. It hadn't been green, more a kind of blond.

Obviously this second piece is from much closer in to the action, but I don't think that's the only reason for the far more embodied – and illicit – sense that the piece now carries. Whereas everything that happened was homogenised, earlier, by the continuous voice of the reflecting narrator, now an immediate contrast is set up between the child in her body, surreptitiously fingering the folds of paper in her tunic, and the nun in hers, drawing lines with a ruler in white chalk on the blackboard. We're perfectly prepared in this way for the primary contrast, between the strangely intimate voice of the priest in the letter, and the nun's voice meting out its dry instructions. The escape from that over-heated room which his words provide is plain to see, as are the implications of the fact that the I-character can repeat them verbatim.

This time, probably because the body is so much more present, there's a furtively erotic quality about the words hidden in her tunic, and a much more potent sense of deeper embroilment to come.

Direct Speech and Relationship

Direct speech also provides a powerful tool for a writer to use to explore relationship. When a scene takes place primarily in the memory of the point of view character, it's easy to gloss over the concerns of whomever else is involved. But when each of the main characters, say, has a voice, the whole complex dynamic of whatever's going on inside of and between them *both* comes into play. By letting your characters speak, you can begin to understand them – and their relationships – as never before.

You can see this writer's understanding of her male character begin to deepen when she starts to give his side of the dialogue in this scene. The first version lets us understand the girl's (the point of view character's) feelings. But Torsten, the male character, remains shadowy.

That night at our daily awards ceremony the coach said, "The surfing prize goes to the only person who drew blood today. It takes a lot for a dumb Canadian to come down here to Australia and try to surf. And she got right back in the water to body surf after." I got a chocolate bar. So I like the name dumb Canadian. Most of my friends call me that sometimes. Their way of claiming me for their own.

I kiss Torsten again. We have the kissing thing figured out now and we fit together real well. I like the feeling of his body on mine. We put our arms around each other but we don't really go much further than this. Sometimes he's touched me over my top but that's it. Sometimes I think we should do more but he won't let me try. He says it's nice just to do this. Just to kiss.

One of my friends from school, one of the guys, tried to tell me once that Torsten was just using me. I laughed and told him if he was I didn't know what for. This didn't seem to satisfy him. I'd been used before. I knew the difference. I wasn't an idiot.

Torsten and I go out for two months. Most days after school we go over to his place for a couple of hours.

But one day he is acting real strange to me at school . He doesn't give me the usual kiss when he first sees me and he just seems strange. A little alarm goes off in my head but I don't want to hear it. I see him talking to my best friend Luciana a couple of times during the day but she doesn't say anything to me about what is going on either.

At the end of the day when we meet up he tells me we have to talk. On no. Not this. I'm too happy.

He tells me something I can't even really remember, I'm not even really listening to everything because all I know is that he is breaking up with me and I don't want this to happen. I don't want him to break up with me. I want to keep kissing and I want to go over to his house and to lie on his bed. I want to hear him play the drums. I don't want him to be like this withdrawing going away gone.

I'm walking across the field, the opposite way from Torsten's house, towards the mall where I know my friends will be hanging out. I'm bawling really loud. I can't help it. I know I shouldn't let him see me bawl this loud god it is embarrassing but I can't help it.

Somewhere in my mind I am thinking that this is what heartbreak feels like. My first love and my first heart break. And though it hurts like hell and completely sucks I think at least it's normal. Normal heartbreak.
(Monique Shebbeare)

There's absolutely no indication, in this scene, of whatever motives Torsten may have for doing what he does. But if this writer puts him on the spot and makes him talk, what will she discover? When she does so, this is what results:

At the end of the day Torsten and I meet up. On the grass at the edge of the quad.

"We need to talk," he says.

Oh no. Not this. I'm so happy. I don't want it to end.

"I've been thinking."

"I know," I say. "You've been avoiding me all day."

"I didn't want to talk to you until I was really sure. I needed to think."

"About what?" I ask. I don't want to know the answer. Not this.

"I'm still in love with Tammy."

Slam. It can't be. But we've been so happy. Haven't we? Was it just me?

146

"And you're going back to Canada soon anyway. And we can still be friends. We'll always be friends. You know that I love you, just not like that."

My hands are shaking. Hold it back. Hold it back. Don't cry. Whatever you do, don't cry. But I always cry. I can't help it. Can't hide it. I just want him to kiss me. I can't say anything. What can I say? I just want to tell him he's wrong. He can't do this.

"Moniquie, you know I love you as a friend. You're a really special girl."

He is just a foot away from me. We stand so close to each other. The school is behind him, the field behind me. I stare at the concrete of the quadrangle, the cafeteria windows. I don't want to look at him. When? I don't get it. When did this happen? It seemed so normal yesterday.

"Is that why you were talking to Luch today?" I ask him.

"Yeah. I knew you'd be hurt. I wanted to ask her what I should do."

"What did she tell you?"

Did she tell him to break up with me? I'm not holding it in very well anymore. The tears have started running down my face and my breath has started to gather in sobs. I try to breathe normally but I can't control it. I'm starting to bawl and it's loud.

"She told me I should talk to you. Tell you the truth. She told me you're really in love with me."

Yeah, I am. Why bother hiding it?

"Please don't cry Moniquie."

"I can't help it." I barely get the words out before another sob catches me. Torsten takes my hand. Pulls me to him. Hugs me.

"Do you think we could kiss, one more time? Just to say goodbye?" he asks.

One more kiss. My face brightens. Of course.

He takes my face in his hands. We move together slowly. Lips touching, tongues together soft like we know how so well now. I want it to last forever. I want to go back to his house, lie on his bed, listen to him play the drums. I wish my kiss could make him change his mind.

It seems to me that we (and doubtless the writer, too) are very much closer to understanding Torsten now. His motives still aren't completely clear, nor do they need to be: she's leaving; he's feeling drawn back to his old girlfriend (maybe *because* she's leaving); he's still drawn to the I-character physically and emotionally, but perhaps he's become aware that he's going to have to go on here after she's gone. Hearing what he

147

says and, perhaps more important, the fact that we can hear *how* he says it, satisfies me as a reader, anyway, that he's not feckless or cruel, but as articulate and as inarticulate as any young person needs to be when he's making choices. His wanting not to upset her, as well as the loud abandon with which she allows herself to be upset, both seem reassuring. These young people are both all right, and they will be all right. It *is* normal heartbreak. They've revealed that to us in the course of their conversation.

Tips on Writing Direct Speech

1. Don't let dialogue make you shift point of view

As you may have noticed in the previous dialogue, it is not necessary (or desirable) to shift the point of view in the story during a verbal exchange between two characters. Although the writer quotes what Torsten says, she never ventures into his mind to tell us what he is thinking. We are told *only* what the I-character thinks, and what she can hear of what he says: we remain, in other words, firmly entrenched within her point of view.

2. Just say "said"

Although it can feel like hopelessly bad writing to keep repeating "said", that word quickly becomes invisible to the reader in a way that "observed", "announced", "opined", and "claimed" never can. "The line of dialogue belongs to the character," as Elmore Leonard puts it, "The verb is the writer sticking his nose in. But said is far less intrusive than grumbled, gasped, cautioned, lied. I once noticed Mary McCarthy ending a line of dialogue with 'she asseverated', and had to stop reading to get the dictionary."[60]

3. Forget the adverbs

A difficult lesson every playwright has to learn is that once the dialogue is down on the page, it's up to someone else – the director or the actor – to interpret it. Stage directions, if they're permissible at all, are kept to a minimum and used mainly for blocking, as the name suggests. The writer's only real control over the *way* someone says something comes from the words themselves: a line of dialogue just has to express anger, for instance, so clearly that there's no other way it can be delivered.

Adverbs are the fiction-writer's attempt to give stage directions, and many would argue that they're equally futile. Let the reader hear your character's tone of voice in *what* that character says, not because you explained how he or she said it. The truth is, it won't work very well anyway. Think of an adverb as the tiniest unit of "telling". As always, it's far more evocative to show.

Writing Experience

FREEFALL WRITING

Continue writing as usual, but whenever speech comes up, turn toward it rather than away. Use direct speech ("he said ...") rather than reported speech ("he said that he ..."). And as always, stay with the precepts: write what comes up, go toward what has energy for you, don't change anything, and give all the sensuous detail.

Writing Tip: Real conversation seldom matches up: people follow their own, often separate, lines of thought in a conversation. Consider what each person really wants out of a conversation and let their words reflect that preoccupation.

TIMED WRITING

Write a ten-minute dialogue (between two people) on each of the following topics:

1. The Same Old Argument
2. Why don't you come out and say what you mean?
3. I know I shouldn't tell you this, but
4. I wish you hadn't told me that
5. Saying goodbye
6. Don't blame me!
7. Put on the spot
8. What were you thinking?

Writing Tip: Try doing these exercises first by writing *only* dialogue (no thoughts, no stage directions). Then try backing one of these dialogues with a completely unrelated scene that has no speech, from somewhere else in your writing, and see what happens.

Chapter Thirteen
Opening Out

At this point, when you look back over your writing, you may be able to see a natural movement toward fully fledged scenes, more showing and less telling, and a greater degree of identification with the characters; all of this comes about spontaneously over time, as a result of your own absorption in what you're writing about. But I've also noticed that this process of moving further into the material as you write can sometimes get slowed down or snagged.

For one thing, I've discovered that people often adopt a habitual distance from whatever it is they're writing about, just as they do from the events that take place in life. It's good to have a way to shift that distance from time to time, because standing back too far can limit your scope. Also, especially when the writing is autobiographical, you may step back, consciously or unconsciously, when a particular subject or technical demand comes up, even when the piece you're writing seems to be calling for you to come in closer.

Because most people seem to benefit from being given a push now and again, I've developed a technique whose purpose is to help writers move past such hesitations and see what happens – a technique I call "opening out". Once again, you'll need to judge for yourself whether doing this feels as if it would be helpful or detrimental to your writing at this stage, and act accordingly. But if, having read what I have to say about it, you are able to identify some places in your writing where it looks to you as if you've held back and open those out, surprising things may happen – things that might have taken a long time to come about in any other way.

What Opening Out Means

To "open out" an area of your writing means to enter into the richness of detail that lies behind something you mentioned only briefly the first time around. You may not have felt you had time to go into whatever it was, or you may not have thought it necessary at the time. But looking back, you may be able to see whether you speed past some of the same areas *every* time – and this is where it gets interesting. Of course it will be significantly easier to see places that could be opened out in your writing partner's work than in your own, and vice-versa. But because it's not easy to get the hang of this the first time around, I'll explain further as I show you some examples.

In the first place, be specific. Choose a specific word or phrase and invite yourself or your partner to open *that* out, rather than naming some general area that could be explored. And in the second, be curious. What was it, reading your partner's piece, that you were left wanting to know more about? Something that left you thinking, "Show me!" That may be your first indication that something was being passed over quickly – something the writer might benefit from opening out.

What you're going to ask yourself, or your partner, to do is to show the specific details that lie behind that word or summary. The object of the exercise is not to improve the piece of writing (though at some time in the future you may want to use it for that purpose). Its purpose is to bring you (or your partner) closer in to the world you're writing about.

Have a look at this writing sample. Then I'll show you what I asked the writer to open out, why, and what happened when she did that.

I sleep on a piece of foam that looks like it's been chewed on, the makeshift bed a urine-yellow, which blends nicely with the puke-green industrial cord and faux wood paneling. It smells down here, like all basements, mouldy wetness and dirty laundry.

It costs $300 a month. Not much really, between tips and my wage I can cover it. My friends think it's cool, a constant party, no parents around to cause problems but what they don't understand is that I have to buy the toilet paper. Do you know how depressing it is to wake up without toilet paper? Oh – and tampons. I have to buy my own fucking tampons. Yeah, it's cool in my parent-free, toilet paper and tampon-free zone.

My schoolmates, my best friend, wake up and have breakfast with their parents. Maybe a little snap, crack, pop before their two-door garage rolls up, like some giant suburban smile, that spits out a car and delivers them to school. Clothes tidy and clean, homework done, and a nice pep talk ending in "atta girl" or "go get 'em tiger". Not for this chick.

I get up from my foam pad, unzip my sleeping bag and eat some dry coffee crystals to get my motor running – I feel just like an astronaut.

I shower in a metal, wait, I think it's tin, phone booth barely large enough to lift up my elbows.

I rub some more coffee crystals on my gums, for the buzz, and say goodbye to all my earwig friends.

<u>Go home? No, all this is still better than home</u>.
(Jennifer Arnold)

For me, the word "home" in this piece virtually had flashing lights around it. What could "home" have been like, to drive this young person (the I-character) to this extreme? It's the hidden Other of the whole piece – a presence by comparison with which everything in this basement room has value. As a reader, I know "home" can't be good, but apart from that, the field is wide open. And because the I-character's persona is somewhat flip and defensive, I'm hoping that when she talks about home, she'll be able to show me what's behind that persona.

So I asked the writer to open out that specific word, "home", and this is what she wrote:

I've made a plan. A plan to make this place more tolerable; first, smile a lot, it seems to keep them both happy. Though, if it were me, I'd be on edge around a fifteen-year-old who smiles constantly. I'd be looking for drugs, roaches hidden not so carefully around the house. What else? Oh yeah, second, if I can at all help it, I shouldn't breathe, think, or speak. I must dry swallow my words, eat them up and push them down. I wonder what Helen Keller's relationship with her mom was like?

So I stand here, washing dishes, listening to music, smiling stupidly at the bubbles in the sink.

"What are you smiling about?"

"Nothing." That's true. Really, my mind is big and blank, like a fart. Usually this conversation goes like "What are you crying about? I'll give you something to cry about!" But now she is mad at me for smiling.

"Turn off that music, it's depressing."

"I'm not depressed," I say flatly, calmly, like I'm talking to a tiger that needs calming.

"Are you being smart?"

"I am smart." Oh no. I'm not being anything. Just let me do the dishes in peace. Already Operation Deaf, Dumb & Blind is in the weeds.

"That music will make you suicidal." She comes nearer, standing beside me at the sink.

"You wish." I'm pleased with my comeback. I can feel the heat rise off her body and touch my arm. I'm pleased with the satisfying sting it leaves behind, making her pink in the face. I turn just in time to catch her hand across my cheek. It burns.

She takes another swing; I catch her hand and throw it back at her. She keeps coming, her arms a windmill. I grab her shoulders, small and narrow like a child, and push her to the floor. Her mouth pops into a doll's "o" of surprise. Her arms and legs sticking out.

Upstairs, I lock the bathroom down. Her hand, small and precise, is imprinted on my face – the blood rushing through the surface, collecting on my skin. I've got to get the swelling down before school.

For me, this opened-out section does exactly what I hoped it would: it vividly shows the sort of home-life to which the earwig-infested basement room is preferable. And it also makes the I-character much more available. The action of the new piece carries the reader straight past that character's defensive persona and into the pain of the situation that lies behind it, all the while sustaining the same talky, ironic, often humourous tone of voice that was one of the real assets of the original piece.

As you'll have noticed with this example, it's not necessary, desirable or usually even possible for what you write in the "opening out" exercise to be somehow retrofitted into the original. Here, the word "home" in the original piece opened out into quite a different subject (the home environment she came from, rather than that of the room she's moved into). The purpose is to take you closer in to some important area of the writing that you didn't explore (for whatever reason) the first time around. Let me give you another example. For this timed exercise, the topic was "Looking for love (in all the wrong places)", the title of a song by Waylon Jennings.

[William] was the hardest knock on my ass and no doubt the most painful because of my age, because of figuring that I would have seen the nose of the train that ran me off the track before it hit me square on and dragged me mercilessly down the rails, until I was able to unleash myself and roll off. I was an adult! I'd been around, but not like this. I hadn't experienced this kind of misconception that was so calculated and so practiced that I didn't see it coming. Love was still in the wrong place, in the mask of tall, dark and handsome, and too nice to imagine could be anything but wonderful. When the truth hit me one night after catching him in an unguarded moment, the reality of his false identity poured out of his mouth as fast as it had come from the bottle. I had the good conscience to run, I had the where-with-all to drag my body down the hall and out the door. There I stood on the other side, shaken and trembling and over-wrought with "how could I's."

As lively as this piece is, the writer is leaving us to take a lot on faith: much is being said that's based on judgments and inferences from data that she doesn't give. Because it felt important for this writer to get beyond the distance created by looking back on this I-character and commenting, I asked her to open out the phrase (now underlined), "catching him in an unguarded moment":

I knocked on his door, heart pounding in anticipation, he wasn't expecting me. I was actually on my way home and then decided to turn around and go see him anyway. The door flung open and as he pulled open the door he fell slightly off balance and knocked himself against the wall "hiiiii …" it was very drawn out and in a voice I didn't recognize. His eyes were wide and darting around me, he was surprised to see me. He stood in the doorway with his shirt off and wearing green sweat pants I had never seen before. Buster was circling around his legs but he wasn't wagging his tail as usual. Buster looked like he was cowering. The air was heavy and thick with discomfort. None of this seemed right. Then he stepped back away from the door and tripped on his own feet. He was drunk, slobbery wet, unleashed, almost falling down drunk. He stumbled down the short hallway towards the kitchen falling against the wall, grabbing the sofa for support. He fell into a chair, legs spread out in front of him, a bottle of wine was open on the table. The glass beside it was almost empty. It was all happening so fast, and I wasn't sure what to think. Everyone gets drunk once in a while … he seemed ok, then he started to speak, or slur, long drawn out rambling sentences that bent themselves into critical accusations with an edge that was cutting through my heart. With each biting slurred sloppy word, my heart began to race. His eyes were black as the night and when I looked into them I saw nothing, the bottom of a well. They were eyes that were closed off from the world, eyes so hollow and desperate, they were falling into the back of his head. My world started spinning around me and I realised I had to get out of there.

You can see at a glance how difficult it would be to fit this piece back into the original. The whole tone is different, as well as the perspective (the writer is now looking directly through the eyes of the I-character, rather than looking back on her from an older, wiser person's perspective). But you can also see immediately how much closer in to her subject the writer has moved – and not just into this particular "unguarded moment", but into the writing in general. It's close up, moment-by-moment. The ironic, self-deprecating voice has vanished.

Recognising Common Areas of Resistance

Emotional Avoidance

Probably the most common reason for avoiding something, at least early on in this writing process, is the fear that a particular subject or aspect of that subject may turn out to be painful to explore. While the act of avoidance itself may be unconscious, it's something you may well be able to see when you look back at the writing.

Although it's hazardous to make inferences about why a writer has written something one way and not another, my hunch is that emotional avoidance might have been behind the narrative distance in this piece:

> *What are we going to put on her gravestone, my sister asked me with despair in her voice. Could we say, "our loving mother lies here"? Deep sadness pushes the word around. Was she a loving mother? The question lies still in a known answer. There is silence in the room as my siblings and I think of the dying woman in the hospital.* <u>*They tell me about sitting beside her and feeling a warm longing thankfulness for seeing her childlike wonder*</u>*. I take it, as my memory is of a dying woman who closes her eyes as she sees her Canadian daughter entering her room. I speak of her anger at me for having been so far away and perhaps for enjoying my life. My siblings nod. Each acknowledges how hard they worked to look after her and how close they feel with each other for having done it so well. I sit and feel my aloneness and my differences and yet I feel close and thankful for their taking on a task I could not have done. My demanding, bible-reading mother lies to rest under a stone that says here lies our beloved mother, beside my beloved father.*

(Simone Fidelman)

Because I couldn't see these siblings except as vague outlines, and could really only guess at their experience in the hospital, I asked this writer to open out the (now underlined) phrase, "They tell me about sitting beside her and feeling a warm longing thankfulness for seeing her childlike wonder."

She wrote:

> *It is quiet in the room.*

My second oldest brother speaks with a low voice. Tears are streaming down his cheeks. "I have never felt this way," he says, his voice sinking even deeper. I have never seen him this way. My heart opens ever so slightly. Why is it so difficult to feel compassion for this tall, awkward moving, balded man? "I held my mother's hand for the first time." His body shifts in a question-like move, his voice trailing in a soft unbelieving crescendo. Did he really? I imagine this brother sitting beside our dying mother and holding her hand. Pictures of her hand, skinny, bony, coloured with a purple ink pen, lying with dying energy in my brother's big, swollen, bursting hands are clicking by as if I am looking into one of those old viewfinders.

My brother's voice fills the room once more. "She smiled," he says. "She smiled at me." I smile too as I see his body lighter and more at ease with the small movements of his speech.

Adults we are, I think, and yet my siblings' faces shine with childlike wonder.

"She was like a child," he continues. It is quiet again, my viewfinder clicks into the most beautiful scene ... my mother, my siblings, me, my father ... are sitting together, holding hands. Sweet compassion is in this room. It holds me ever so tenderly.

You have only to compare this piece with the previous one to see how the writer's response to the opening out exercise has brought these people much more fully present in the room, and perhaps even more important, brought the process of discovery in that moment present on the page, instead of leaving it encapsulated among the I-character's various memories. It's as if something that wasn't complete in my experience of the subject is complete now – it has come into being on the page. That's something I often feel when a missing piece has been successfully opened out.

Technical Avoidance

Although it's often hard to separate this kind of hesitation from emotional avoidance, I frequently have the sense that someone may be avoiding something she or he is not sure of being able to accomplish in writing. Most of us come to moments when we're not sure we're good enough writers to show a certain thing, so we try to dodge it by summarising, instead.

This writer, for instance, creates an evocative summary of a long-ago trip to Ceylon, and I don't think any kind of emotional avoidance informs her decision to move as quickly as she does across the territory. My guess is that, in the moment of writing, she may have thought that to convey this young person's experience of a whole country was a big job, and the best way to do it might be to touch on as many incidents and impressions as possible, in quick succession. Perhaps you can get a sense of the speed of that movement from this excerpt:

We swim in water that is as warm as our skin, watching tiny fish dart around us. In the distance fishermen sing ancient songs as they hurl nets like lassoes. I want to stay in this paradise forever.

In the market I buy glass bangles and gaudy earrings. The Pereiras' servant Subha takes me to a tailor who measures me for sari blouses. "You are big girl," he says, pinching my arm and lingering with his tape-measure just a little too long over my chest.

I buy two saris, one an everyday one in mauve cotton, and the other emerald green silk with gold threads. It's expensive but I love it. When the blouses are finished Subha shows me how to drape the sari, folding it carefully over the long petticoat. The blouses are tight but that is the way they are made, I'm told, to emphasise the bust.

Before we leave the island I wear the green sari and the glass bangles and the garish earrings to a party in the hills. It's a strange gathering of Colombo socialites who call each other dear chap and old fellow and Dickie or Fatty. They admire us four tourist girls decked out in our saris and ask the same old questions about kangaroos and how much everything costs in Australia. Some talk about back home and I realise they mean England. Most are burghers, mixed-race. One woman tells me she can't wait to get out of this place. I want to tell her I want to stay here forever. We could swap.
(Ann de Hugard)

Does moving on this rapidly qualify as "technical avoidance"? If this writer doubted her ability to do more than that, it would. Whatever the case, when I had read the paragraph that summed up the "strange gathering of Colombo socialites", I realised that I still had no real idea as to what the I-character found "strange" about it. Clearly there was more in her mind's eye than was making it onto the page. So that sentence struck me as a good site for an experiment: what would this writer learn if she tried to enter what led this young woman to come to that conclusion?

Here is what she wrote:

The party is at a huge bungalow in the hills, our hosts friends of the Pereiras, Dickie and Dottie. I don't catch their surnames, everyone speaks so fast here.

We all troop in and conversation stops. The living room is more like a ballroom – huge with polished floors and rattan furniture arranged casually.

"Planters Punch, ladies?" Dickie calls to us. We nod in unison and he snaps his fingers at a polished waiter in a snappy uniform, turban and all. Like the ones at Galle Face Hotel. Maybe they've hired him for the night.

The waiter brings us the drinks on a silver tray. I take one and inspect it. On the top of the glass is a sliver of pineapple and a Chinese umbrella. I take a sip – coconut, rum and pineapple juice all in one mouthful. I want the recipe.

By now we're surrounded by Dottie's pals all admiring our outfits. "Love your sari, dear," a fat woman says. Her bare midriff bulges between her turquoise blouse and sari and her gold bangles strain against the rolls of fat on her arm. "How much did you pay?"

I know what's coming so I quickly make a calculation. "A hundred and fifty," I say. I've taken off twenty five.

She tut tuts and frowns and turns to a friend. "Too much." She shakes her head. "Next time you must come with me, darling. I know the best places. Bargaining's not for everyone. They sniff out the tourists from miles away." She tut tuts again and waddles off.

I turn to Judy. "I thought I did well. Subha did the bargaining."

Judy laughs. "Stuck up bitch."

Dickie approaches. "Fill up, girls?"

I shake my head. "I'm fine thanks for the moment."

He stands there, white safari suit jacket straining across fat belly. Sweat beads his brow. "Jolly hot night," he says, "even for the hills."

I'm feeling cool, the fan above our heads swinging and swaying. Or is it me? I take another swig and drain my glass. "I will have another, thanks."

Dickie clicks his fingers and the waiter comes running. "How much would you pay for a cocktail in Aussie?" Dickie asks Judy.

"I don't really know," she says. "Actually I prefer beer."

He giggles, leering at her, his little eyes squinting.

From this colourful scene with its sparky dialogue, I get first-hand experience of the mixture of admiration and condescension – on both sides, perhaps – that led that young woman to think of this gathering as "strange". I'm starting to find it almost as fascinating as she does. Even more important, this writer has now found herself capable of conveying this world, with all its contradictions, close up, in a much more intimate, complex and dramatic way. If she can proceed from scene to scene, each one as close up and moment-by-moment as this, she will have taken us inside this country in a way that no summary, however vivid, ever could. We will then be left with the sense of having experienced this world just as the main character did – of having lived through her experiences there as her, which for a great many readers of memoir and fiction is surely the goal.

So when a sense of the difficulty of your subject makes you draw back and resort to a summary, bear in mind that a single scene will immediately show more than a summary ever can. It's the proverbial picture that's worth a thousand words. Take the plunge and risk entering into the heart of it. You'll find you're more than capable of showing what transpires there.

And there's an added bonus you may not be expecting: that's where the fun begins.

Picking Through the Strata

Although I could continue to give you examples for a long time to come, you'll find equally good places to open out in your own writing. Look for opportunities in the places I've suggested – and of course there are others. Some people habitually end a piece just when things are beginning to happen, so that the last sentence becomes a good place to open out. Some take too big a jump (I think of it as "telescoping") from one sentence to the next, and create a much wider gap than a reader can leap with any confidence. For the most part, the places of avoidance are highly idiosyncratic, but they are none the less important for that. "Opening out" holds the key, in my view, to an important stage in a writer's progress. It's a matter of becoming aware of some old patterns, so that you can push through them and engage even more deeply with your writing.

Writing Experience

FREEFALL WRITING

Continue to write as usual, coming as close in as possible to the parts that have the most energy for you. Be aware, as you write, if there is any area of what arises for you that you're avoiding, and try to move into it. But above all, stay with the precepts: write what comes up for you, don't change anything, give all the sensuous detail.

Writing Tip: "Overwhelm" is most likely to occur when the material is too recent. If you can't find your way through the welter of detail, consider the possibility that the material may not have composted sufficiently, even if it *is* more than ten years old. If it insists on being written anyway, don't forget how much one picture can show. Pick whatever detail has the most energy for you, and open that out. One step at a time. Slow, slow is fast.

TIMED WRITING

Re-read your earliest Freefall Writing (or that of your writing partner) to find the places that seem important to open out. Underline the specific word, phrase or sentence to be opened out. Spend 20 minutes opening out that underlined passage in writing. Do this with eight passages over the month to come.

Writing Tip: As you re-read your writing, take note of the critical voices (the Dragons) that speak to you. Keep a record of what they say. This is another excellent chance to become familiar with their messages.

Chapter Fourteen
Freefalling with Intention

A question I frequently hear asked about this process (though primarily from people who have just begun) is: "How much writing do I have to do in this way before I can start writing fiction/memoir/creative non-fiction?"

I can understand where the question comes from. All writers, even those in their twenties, evidently, seem to feel the same urgency to get their work out to the reading public, the same fear that they've already waited too long. The wolves of comparison are snapping at the runners of their sleigh, and there's no one left in the bridal party to throw overboard but themselves. Spending months or even a year or two writing Freefall when they could be writing a novel, say, sounds like nothing but a blueprint for frustration.

When most people discover what writing in this way has to offer, that sense of urgency recedes. But before long there's the mounting pile of Freefall stories behind them. What do they do with them? Are they short stories already? And if not, why aren't they? What would make them into stories? Novels? Can't all of this writing add up to a novel in itself?

163

To answer these questions appropriately, it's important to distinguish first between this way of writing as a process and the (often autobiographical) writing it produces. The writing you do in this spontaneous way can be thoroughly engaging to a reader and not infrequently proves to be publishable – a matter I will discuss further on in this chapter. But by far the most important thing about this process is the *experience of writing* to which you become accustomed. Freefall is not a tool to be put aside when you move on to other things, but rather a way of surrendering into the act of creation that will be your chief source of new material – not to mention enjoyment – throughout your writing life.

So the real question is not "How long do I have to write Freefall?" but "When can I bring in more intention?" And the answer: the stronger your ability to surrender has grown, the more intention it's able to sustain.

Here's what the gradual re-introduction of intention into your writing can look like. In the beginning, when you still have a virtual stranglehold on your writing, the amount of intention you bring to it needs to be very small. You're learning surrender in the act of writing – and just following the precepts is enough. The more you write in this way, the easier it becomes for you to relax into the writing and allow yourself to become absorbed. As a result, you learn what are considered "skills" in writing: to enter into the perspective of your character, to show more and summarise less, to give moment-by-moment scenes, and to include dialogue – not inhibiting your absorption by doing these things, but rather, as we have seen demonstrated, intensifying it.

As you continue, you begin to find that you're curious about, and can bring in, further refinements, still without interrupting your absorption – further considerations of craft. And so the balance between will and surrender continues to shift, as you discover what you need to know, find out, and let the writing show you how to use it.

This whole process of bringing more direction into your writing feels, once you're ready for it, like simply deepening what you can hold in the field of your awareness, as you write. But what's crucial is never to lose touch with the open heart and receptivity that lies at the heart of your experience of writing: the Freefall.

Because the surrendered state in which you've learned to write will always be the engine of creativity that drives your experience, it's very important to safeguard it. You can do that by making sure you're really ready to bring in more intention – or, to put it another way, by finding out *who* wants the writing to become more purposeful: the writer in you, or one of your Inner Critics.

Here is a brief inventory that can help you to discern that. Do you look forward to writing? When something arises for you to fall into, do you readily become absorbed in it? When something comes up that you think may be difficult to write about, do you tend to "go fearward"? Can you easily supply specific, sensuous details as the need arises? Are you comfortable writing dialogue? Does the writing sometimes take you somewhere that surprises you?

If your answer to most of these questions is no, or even a strong sense of unease, it may not be time for you to distract yourself by bringing any more baggage into the act of writing than the simple intention to be fully present for whatever comes up. I would recommend instead that you continue to practise the suggestions made in these chapters. To tamper with the vital progress you've already made in learning to forget yourself in writing might be too great a risk to take for the time being.

Don't forget: this is not a matter of success and failure, or even of "progress" as that word is usually understood. Your own spontaneous writing may already be "better" (if by that we mean more publishable) than someone else's carefully polished short story. But if it is not a process you can relax into, then you probably need to do more of it.

Autobiography and Fiction

For people whose writing up to this point has been chiefly based in autobiography, the notion of shifting into outright fiction can feel unnerving. And again, I would say, if that thought causes you unease, you may not have done enough Freefall Writing yet. The very skills you are developing – of absorption in your character's viewpoint, of inventing the specifics and the dialogue of the scenes that come up – are central to writing fiction, which is simply going to demand of you that you invent *more*.

But for now, why not keep going as you are for a while longer, playing with the odd "what if", if one occurs to you? To borrow one of the wisdom-sayings from meditation: "How do you keep a sheep from escaping? Give it all the room it needs." The would-be fiction writer who has written enough autobiographical material moves on, still writing what he or she "knows", to be sure, but no longer fettered by the need to rely on a sense of what he or she believes happened in the past.

I know, however, that many people also wonder, given the success they've had with autobiographical writing: couldn't that just go on in another guise? Couldn't autobiography simply be disguised, to become fiction?

Unfortunately, it's not as simple as that. Between autobiography and fiction there are enormous differences. In autobiography, life is the constant referent. Whatever use the writer decides to make of the events that happened, the fact that *they happened* remains their underlying justification, and as readers, we refer to that premise repeatedly as we read. In fiction, events make sense not in relation to life, but to one another. We are aware, as we read fiction, that those events have been included *for a reason*. They constitute a self-consistent world that somehow makes sense – a world that "though [it] has not been explained," to use E.M. Forster's phrase, "is explicable."[61]

Sooner or later, therefore, the choice arises: do you want to write autobiography or fiction? Of course, you can do both. And of course, it's a continuum. There are fictionalised autobiographies and autobiographical fictions, and all the degrees from fact to pure invention in between. Even when a writer intends to write pure fiction, autobiographical facts, characters and events usually find their place in it. But if what you have been writing is largely autobiographical, and your aim is to write fiction, then wait until you become curious about what constitutes a novel or a short story. It's good to be aware of the range of what's been done, so that you can make informed choices. And then you'll need to begin, as you can, to free yourself from the constraints of real life and create a self-consistent world in your writing. If you're writing fiction, you are no longer simply following life; you're writing to show something in particular *about* life.

Remember that the process is a gradual one. You're already inventing scenes, dialogue, and investing yourself in a character. You've already gone a long way, in other words, toward writing fiction. If you're truly curious about other ways to do what you're already doing, have a look at some books by people who have spent time cataloguing a range of possible techniques.[62] If, however, books so exclusively devoted to intention make "a coldness come about [your] heart",[63] put them back on the shelf. You already have the depth of your own experience of writing to fall back on. If you persist, it will show you how to keep widening the scope of what you can do, regardless of what you read.

Do Freefall Stories Have a Future?

What about the "products" of this way of writing – those spontaneous, often autobiographical stories that arise in keeping with the first precept: write what comes up for you. Do they have a future? Are they publishable, and if not, what would make them so?

The answer to these questions, too, depends in part on how far along you are in the process. The whole point of this approach to writing is that it works as a progression: you write one story, then another, then another, increasing in skill and scope as you go. When you look back at a story from the level of skill you've acquired by writing many others since, you have a completely different sense of what revising that story means. You're no longer trying to solve the problem at the level of the problem, but coming back to it from a wholly different level of achievement.

An unusual number of the stories written in this way do have the kind of power and immediacy that would make them absorbing for any reader, and therefore potentially publishable. But it's important to bear in mind that to the extent that your stories are autobiographical, they are not fiction. Simply changing the names or locations, or shifting the point of view from "I", to "he" or "she", won't make them into fiction, which has its own quite different logic, as I've pointed out. One option, then, is to consider their merit as memoir – individually, or linked as a volume if they cover an extended period of time.

Unless you are already famous in a way that would make your life the subject of curiosity, the fact that this work is about your life *per se* will not hold too much intrinsic interest outside your immediate circle. But if there is a unique angle that would stimulate some curiosity in the general public, your work has a good chance of offering the kind of reading that many book-buyers are looking for, and quite a few people have had success publishing their autobiographical Freefall in this way.

Another option is to explore your stories with an eye to discerning their purpose. In my view, the stories which come up when you write this way come up for a reason, and if you, as the writer, can treat them simply as material, you may be able to discern what they show about life, and to revise them with an eye to furthering that purpose. To do this, you need to be able to disengage from "what happened", and this skill may take some time to develop. But once you can do so, you may very well be able to re-cast the same material in such a way that it does work as fiction.

My suggestion, if you would like to discern the "starter-dough" in what you've written, is that you leave the material for long enough that you've almost forgotten writing it. Then look back, to see if you can tell what it was you found arresting about this series of events in the first place – what made it "come up", when you sat down to write. Once you've felt (or written) your way into what's there, you will begin to discover what else it needs, and in this way the story can grow. Once you can grow a story in that way, there's no limit to the places from which you can draw your material. You're now at a stage where you already *know how to write*. On the next phase of your journey – and it's an exciting one – you will discover what direction you want that ability to take.

The Pleasure of Writing

For those of you who are truly ready to make that shift, a whole new kind of pleasure awaits you. From now on, in your writing life, you will be playing on the edge of a paradox – both holding some intention, and surrendering into the unknown. The internal witness you have been developing, through your earlier writing, is now ready: to know and not know; to engage and stand above. It won't always be easy, but it *will* always be interesting. Often, it will be fascinating. Sometimes, as this writer reports, it will even be "thrilling":

Before, when I would freefall, the writing would keep looping out and out, until sometimes, I'd lose the thread. Not always. But it always seemed so rich and productive. This, I think, is exactly as it should be with freefall in the beginning - just following the scent and seeing where it leads. And it may go all over the place. But, with the chapters - with a piece that's coming together in a novel - I can now see how you can freefall totally - but it's a different knack. You have one foot in the camp of knowing more or less where you're going and who the characters are, etc, and one foot in the "not knowing" camp, where you just freefall into it. Basically, I'm learning to just place myself in a scene and leap off. This is thrilling because I can see the ground coming up and the parachute does get me there without crashing. (I think I was concerned before that it would waft me out to sea, which wasn't, necessarily, the safest place to land.)
(Rosemary Stevens)

And no matter how much you know, you'll always be simply present, simply writing, simply discovering the next sentence.

No matter what degree of intention you bring to that process, the basic ground of your being as a writer is now beneath you – the ability to be fully present with yourself in the moment of creativity and to witness with a trusting mind what transpires there. The longer you write, the further the process will lead you into the uniqueness of voice and authority in writing that is yours alone: something occurs to you, you write it down, and that leads to the next thing that comes along.

Curiously, when I'm around people who are writing in this surrendered way, even when they've just begun, I feel – I think we can all feel – a degree of the same sort of heightened energy that I experienced to such an overwhelming degree in those early days at Cambridge. Although I can't claim to understand it fully, it seems to have to do with their becoming more of who they are. Certainly their voice – the deeper current of their being that can be glimpsed in the writing from the very beginning – becomes steadily stronger as they write this way. And they seem to become kinder, more generous and more capable of deep listening. It may be simply that these writers are now freely engaged in making what Viktor Frankl has called "the one right choice"[64] in each moment. They're writing from a place of greater wholeness, and so at last they're home.

Writing Experience

FREEFALL WRITING

It may be time for you to do some experimenting in writing with intention. After your next writing session, ask yourself, "What happened next?" Experiment with carrying on the story from the point at which you left it. If you feel you've gained something by doing this, continue the experiment.

Writing Tip: In the shift from doing something unconsciously to doing it consciously, it's not unusual to pass through a stage of self-consciousness. If you find that that's the case when you begin to direct your writing, be patient. This too will pass, and the act of writing will feel natural and absorbing once again.

TIMED EXERCISES

1. *Finding the Conflict*
Go back over your writing and locate some area of conflict. Give yourself 20 minutes to write a scene centred specifically in each area of conflict.

2. *Finding the Subject*
Have a look for some recurring subject-areas in your writing (the contrast between power and powerlessness, for example, or belonging and not belonging). Make the label you give to that subject, the topic for your next timed-writing exercise, and give yourself 20 minutes to write the scene. Do this with several scenes from several different subject-areas.

3. *Extending the Story*
Take any piece of writing you have done, and allow yourself 20 minutes to write the next scene that occurred, after the one where you left off.

4. Finding the Characteristic

Looking at your writing, name a few of the prominent characteristics of some of your characters. Turn those characteristics into topics ("Bossy", "Insecure", "Reckless", "Charming") and write a 15-minute scene generated by that topic. (NB: The scene doesn't need to contain that character.)

Writing Tip: One of the virtues of this way of writing is that it shows you how to *write* your way into a story, rather than to *think* your way into one. But if you do find yourself with an idea you want to explore, turn your notion into a topic and do a timed writing piece. It's an excellent way to bypass the thinking mind, and gain access to what the writer in you has to say.

NOTES

INTRODUCTION

1. "Freefall Writing", the name I use to refer both to this way of writing and to the writing it produces, derives from the writing studio led by W.O. Mitchell at the Banff School of Fine Arts in the 1980s. As students there, we were told that the term "free-fall" had been applied by Sandra Jones, a former student and an assistant in the programme, to what Mitchell considered "a kind of free-association or automatic writing". (Barbara & Ormond Mitchell, *W.O. : The Life of W.O. Mitchell* Toronto: M&S, 1999, 2). Mitchell himself claimed he preferred to call his approach "Mitchell's Messy Method". Although my own approach to writing and thus what I mean by "Freefall" is rather different, I have continued the use of the term in my own way, out of gratitude for Mitchell's encouragement and for what I learned at Banff. Where Mitchell's approach is referred to specifically, it will be referenced in the text.

CHAPTER 1

2. W.B. Yeats, "The Circus Animals' Desertion", *The Collected Poems of W.B. Yeats* (London: Macmillan, 1981, 1933) 392.

CHAPTER 2

3. Naomi Epel, *Writers Dreaming* (Melbourne: Bookman Press, 1993) 141-142.
4. "The Unvarnished Truth", *The Weekend Australian*, October 3-4, 2009.
5. *The San Francisco Chronicle*, February 5, 2008.
6. *The Writer's Chapbook: A Compendium of Fact, Opinion, Wit, and Advice from the 20th Century's Preeminent Writers* ed. George Plimpton (New York: Viking, 1989) 60.
7. Preface to *Six Degrees of Separation* by John Guare (New York: Dramatists Play Service Inc., 1992, 1990) 5.

8. Theodore Roethke, "The Waking", *The Waking: Poems, 1933 – 1953* (New York: Doubleday, 1953) 120. (The original line reads, "I learn by going where I have to go.")

CHAPTER 3

9. William Stafford, *Writing the Australian Crawl: Views on the Writer's Vocation* (Ann Arbor: The University of Michigan Press, 1986, 1978) 18.
10. Natalie Goldberg, *Writing Down the Bones: Freeing the Writer Within* (Boston: Shambhala, 1986) 14.
11. *Writing the Australian Crawl*, 17.
12. "Sensuous" was W.O. Mitchell's word for this sort of detail. This precept derives from advice he gave us, as does the fifth (the so-called "Ten-Year Rule").
13. I see this surprising fact about writing reflected in Roland Barthes' observation that, "The pleasure of the text is that moment when my body pursues its own ideas – for my body does not have the same ideas I do" (*The Pleasure of the Text* trans. Richard Miller (New York: Farrar, Strauss and Giroux, Inc., 1975) 17).
14. Robert Burdette Sweet, *Writing Towards Wisdom: The Writer as Shaman* (Carmichael CA: Helios House, 1990) 17.
15. Ibid, 21.
16. Ibid, 21.
17. Julia Cameron, *The Artist's Way: A Spiritual Path to Higher Creativity* (London: Pan Books, 1995, 1994). Cameron suggests that, as preparation for writing, people write three pages each morning of anything that comes to mind.
18. *Writing Down the Bones*, 11–13.
19. Ibid, 14.
20. According to some neuroscientists, we don't store whole memories – just certain "key features" (Rick Hanson with Richard Mendius, *Buddha's Brain: The Practical Neuroscience of Happiness, Love and Wisdom* (Oakland: New Harbinger Publications, 2009) 70). So I suggest you think of yourself as creating that memory as you write, since that may be what's happening anyway. In that context, "I don't remember" becomes a comment from your Inner Critic, to be put aside as you write.

CHAPTER 4

21. *The Writers' Chapbook*, 85.
22. Frank Sheehan, "The Orchard by Drusilla Modjeska", *The Good Book by Frank Sheehan: A Monthly Newsletter of Book Reviews*.
23. *The New Yorker*, August 21, 1989, 23.

CHAPTER 5

24. This distinction was first explicitly drawn by Percy Lubbock, in *The Craft of Fiction* (London: Jonathan Cape, 1972, 1921) 62. ("The art of fiction does not begin until the novelist thinks of his story as a matter to be *shown*, to be so exhibited that it will tell itself.") Virginia Woolf and E.M. Forster both took vigorous public exception to Lubbock's book, not because of this dictate (which both of them followed instinctively), but because Lubbock had had the temerity, in this and other matters, to say what a writer "must" do.
25. Jacques Lacan, *Écrits: A Selection* trans. Alan Sheridan (London: Tavistock Publications, 1977) 77.
26. Suffragist campaign slogan attributed to Nellie McClung, 1915.

CHAPTER 6

27. *The Writer's Chapbook*, 29.
28. This whole arc of experience in writing, in which what is unknown makes itself known, is what led Harlan Ellison, I think, to say that "writing entails the ongoing courage for self-discovery. It means one will walk forever on the tightrope, with each new step presenting the possibility of learning a truth about oneself that is too terrible to bear." ("How I Write" *Writer's Digest* December, 1995, 30.)

CHAPTER 7

29. Private correspondence, January 11, 1996.
30. Mario Vargas Llosa, *A Writer's Reality*, ed. Myron I. Lichtblau (Boston: Houghton Mifflin Company, 1992) 79-80.
31. "The New Biography", *Collected Essays: Volume Four* (London: The Hogarth Press, 1967, 1923) 235.
32. Ibid, 234.
33. Sharon Butala, "Telling the Truth", *Brick* 4 (Summer 1994), 50.

34. This phrase is the title of a book of poems by Lorna Crozier (Toronto: M&S, 1985).

35. Janet Burroway, *Writing Fiction: A Guide to Narrative Craft* (New York: Harper Collins, 1992) 61.

36. This writer went on to publish a book of stories about this time-period entitled *Another World*.

37. E.M. Forster, *Aspects of the Novel*, ed. Oliver Stallybrass, Penguin Classics (London: Penguin Books, 2000, 1927) 62-63.

38. Lois Phillips Hudson, *Reapers of the Dust: A Prairie Chronicle* (St. Paul: Minnesota Historical Society Press, 1984) xiv.

CHAPTER 8

39. "What Is Real?" *Making It New: Contemporary Canadian Stories* ed. John Metcalf (Toronto: Methuen, 1982) 225.

40. *Six Degrees of Separation*, 5.

41. *The Burning Library: Essays by Edmund White* ed. David Bergman (New York: Vintage, 1995, 1994) npn.

42. Florida Scott-Maxwell, *The Measure of My Days* (New York: Penguin Books, 1979, 1968) 42.

43. Ted Solotaroff, "Writing in the Cold", *Granta* 15 (1985) 270.

44. This theory was developed by Heinz Kohut, who posited that children who do not get enough mirroring are at risk of developing narcissistic personalities later in life. *(The Analysis of the Self: A Systematic Analysis of the Treatment of the Narcissistic Personality Disorders)*

CHAPTER 9

45. "The Notebooks of Malte Laurids Brigge", *The Selected Poetry of Rainer Maria Rilke*, ed. and trans. Stephen Mitchell, Vintage International (New York: Random House, 1989) 95.

46. *Writing Down the Bones*, 3.

47. Natalie Goldberg, *Wild Mind: Living the Writer's Life* (New York: Bantam Books, 1990) 136.

48. "The Four-Fold Way®", *Angeles Arrien: Walking the Mystical Path with Practical Feet*, 2012, http://www.angelesarrien.com.

49. *Writers Dreaming*, 142.

50. "For Authors, Fragile Ideas Need Loving Every Day", *Writers [on Writing]: Collected Essays from The New York Times,* Times Books (New York: Henry Holt and Company, 2001), 161.

51. Ibid, 163.

52. Ibid, 164.

53. Ibid, 163.

54. "The Four-Fold Way®", *Angeles Arrien: Walking the Mystical Path with Practical Feet.*

55. Ibid.

CHAPTER 10

56. Reprinted in John Ciardi and Miller Williams, *How Does a Poem Mean? Second Edition* (Boston: Houghton Mifflin Company, 1975) 172. I recommend John Ciardi's sprightly and insightful first edition of *How Does a Poem Mean?* (1959), unfortunately much obscured in this second edition.

57. "Two Aspects of Language and Two Types of Aphasic Disturbances", *Fundamentals of Language* (Gravenhage: Mouton & Co, 1956) 64.

CHAPTER 11

58. *The Art of Fiction: Notes on Craft for Young Writers* (New York: Random House, 1991, 1984) 97.

CHAPTER 12

59. *Wild Mind,* 203.

60. "Writers on Writing; Easy on the Adverbs, Exclamation Points and Especially Hooptedoodle", *The New York Times,* July 16, 2001.

CHAPTER 14

61. *Aspects of the Novel,* 69.

62. Three books you may find helpful, depending on your level of interest, are (in order of increasing complexity): Jack M. Bickham, *The 38 Most Common Fiction Writing Mistakes* (Cincinnati: Writer's Digest Books, 1997, 1992); Jack Hodgins, *A Passion for Narrative: A Guide for Writing Fiction* (Toronto: M&S, 1993); David Madden, *Revising Fiction: A Handbook for Writers* (New York: Barnes & Noble Books, 2002, 1988).

63. Brenda Ueland, *If You Want to Write: A Book about Art, Independence and Spirit* (Saint Paul: Graywolf Press, 1987, 1938) 167.
64. Viktor Frankl, *Man's Search for Meaning* trans. Ilse Lasch (Boston: Beacon Press, 2006, 1959) 77.